THE PHILOSOPHY OF WONDER

CORNELIS VERHOEVEN

The Philosophy
of Wonder

Translated by Mary Foran

THE MACMILLAN COMPANY, NEW YORK, NEW YORK

CONTENTS

6

One

WONDER AND KNOWLEDGE

1. Introduction

In a book entitled *An Introduction to Philosophy* one might come across a paragraph like this:

> According to Plato, wonder is the beginning of philosophy. Wonder at the changing nature of things led him to assume the existence of eternal, imperishable, and transcendent Ideas which underlie the existence and knowledge of earthly things. When man looks at things, they remind him of the Ideas contemplated by the soul before its union with the body.

Such a paragraph might also have a place in any short history of philosophy. Wonder is central to philosophy, not only as a starting point but also as a principle and a foundation from which everything else proceeds.

This is one viewpoint with regard to philosophy and wonder—Plato's viewpoint. Anyone who familiarizes himself with what has just been said has learned something about Plato and something about philosophy. A little has been added to his general education. Since what has been said here about Plato is correct, one cannot assert that the additional information it gives us has no value as knowledge. To retain something which is not incorrect is a form of knowing.

The question is, Have we thereby been introduced to philosophy? For that matter, if we were aware of all the statements made by all the philosophers of all time, or had an exact knowledge of all philosophical terms in all their meanings, have we thereby been introduced to philosophy? The answer is No. We have been introduced to and are at home in that which philosophy has left behind, what might be called the institutional framework of philosophy or, more harshly, the ashes of its passing. Philosophy is not knowledge of these ashes. An introduction to philosophy does not consist in holding out a handful for inspection, while keeping in reserve an entire mountain for more advanced pupils. Philosophy is not knowledge; as a form of desire (love) it is more a pathos, a state, than an actual knowing. Plato gives this pathos a name: wonder. If philosophy proceeds from wonder, then it proceeds from it completely and in every one of its manifestations. Every philosophical term that has not become mere ashes conveys the pathos of wonder. Every philosophical step forward must be a step backward in the direction of this pathos; every path toward established knowledge must be approached in its light. If wonder is the beginning and principle of philosophy, then wonder will keep its grasp.

I say *if* because I now proceed assuming this is in fact so. For there is another viewpoint that would describe philosophy as a continual victory over and escape from the pathos of wonder. Wonder is not "principle" that, once accepted, can be logically developed. If philosophy begins in wonder it remains as a form of desire, obstinately close to all that this desire arouses. It can be satisfied only by its own hunger; it lives not by possession and conquest but through its own boundless perspectives which it ceaselessly expands.

To introduce someone to philosophy is not to show him

a stretch of the road and then to indicate expansively how that road continues. It means halting where this exploratory path begins and where all others begin; it means practicing philosophy at the place where philosophy begins and ends. The whole history of philosophy lies in a broad circle about the loose space of wonder, even when this wonder is regarded only as a starting point. What cannot be approached from there is not philosophy, however important it may be.

Everything attainable from that point *is* philosophy and is mutually connected. Via this central point all philosophical themes are interrelated. The choice of theme is thus of little importance in philosophy. Whatever does not deal with everything, taking wonder as its starting point, deals with nothing from the philosophical point of view. An introduction could begin just as well with the *cogito* of Descartes as with the Ideas of Plato. It just so happens that from the historical standpoint Plato has priority. This is our thesis: philosophy is a radicalization of wonder in all directions. But radicalization is a slow process and we are necessarily obliged to work the same ground over and over again. Only in this way can the process continue and only thus can it realize its total potential.

An introduction to philosophy is an introduction to the wonder that makes philosophy move. Without this movement, philosophy is merely an institution with which we become acquainted from the outside as curious tourists or, taking the inside view, as mere office clerks. An introduction to philosophy is not the transmission of knowledge that will make a man a philosopher, for philosophy is not the fruit of the possession of any particular knowledge. It is not founded on knowledge nor has it knowledge as its goal. Rather is it an obstinate ignorance, as in Socrates the art of avoiding institutionalized and certain knowledge. Knowledge leads to science, not to philosophy. Science has a firm grasp of reality which it uses as its tool. In this operation, as endorsed by the data of reality, scientific knowledge is verifiable. It can be expanded by hypotheses and experiments. But philosophy is not a science; it is not a means of transmitting knowledge. It is what it is before it can be termed knowledge. There is a knowledge of philosophy that is not philosophy, a knowledge of the many statements made by the many philosophers in the course of the centuries. This knowledge in itself is not philosophy although it can be the gateway to it. One can be moved to philosophy by making a thorough study of these statements. Yet even this is a form of motion, a pathos, a leap from knowledge into unknowing, the endless deferment of certitude. A philosophic statement must be set in motion, brought back again to its basic inspiration, if it is to move us to philosophy. An acquaintance with these statements is to a certain extent desirable since the thoughts and questions of the philosophers who have gone before us help to determine our own position in the process of a continuing philosophical inquiry. But the essential thing is always something other than mere familiarity.

In wonder everything is at stake. Though modest in appearance, its pursuit is a massive undertaking in which no stone is left unturned. Would an introduction to it be like an introduction to a particular science, a provisional orientation to the essential aspects of that science? If so, wonder would have to be something in which some have progressed further than an introduction, to a total, exhaustive investigation. Wonder then would only be a knowledge of wonder, not a pathos. An introduction to the study of law is intended only for beginners; those who are already at home in it need meatier stuff. Thus the beginner's situation is clearly different from the expert's, who already feels at home in his subject.

Yet one can be introduced to a subject or situation only if one is capable of feeling more or less at home in it afterward. But can a man feel at home everywhere after a simple introduction? This depends on the nature of the house to which the introduction gives access and the manner in which it must be lived in. Some houses are ready-made whereas others must first be built by the occupant, and only become homes by the fact of occupation. A person can be at home in the first house once he is introduced

there, but this "feeling at home" only attains a certain degree of intensity, roughly comparable to that experienced in
an hotel. He knows his way around, but he is not the occupant. In the second house a person is not yet at home on
being introduced; in actual fact the home does not yet exist.
It becomes a home only when he feels at home there and in
the measure in which he is capable of being at home in it.
At most then the introduction can merely hope to have inspired the person introduced to make his home in the house.

Even so, all this is based on the assumption that the
house exists in some form or other and that occupancy is
possible. An introduction to philosophy as a history and an
institution is possible on these grounds, but not an introduction to wonder. Wonder is not a house in which it is
possible to live; it is not even a well-defined state. It is, in
a way, the opposite of familiarity and thus hardly a condition one could be introduced to: it would require that a man
be extra-duced from his sense of being at home. It is this
contrast between the words extra-duce and introduce that
suddenly reveals the verbal character of introduction. Introduction is not contemplation but action; it leads to something, sets somebody in motion, may even startle him.
Wonder is not something that can be set out for display and
then mastered. It has to be aroused. This means that an introduction to wonder is of a special type.

Like pathos, wonder is granted or inflicted; it cannot be
incited voluntarily from within. In this matter, the intro-
ducer's function is to inspire rather than to inform, so that
what he does arouses that which he is introducing. His
function is to elicit wonder as a response to, and as an element in, an existence full of things that are taken for
granted. This is naturally a risky undertaking, for not only
is it difficult to do this without lapsing into pseudo-lyricism
but it must also be assumed that a mind can be induced to
wonder only in the measure in which it can assimilate it,
in other words, in which it can absorb the shock that
wonder causes. Beyond this measure an agogic activity is
useless.

Anyone who goes about incautiously inciting to wonder will probably not see this wonder lead to philosophy. It either stagnates in an infertile amazement or else, and this is more probable, he himself is regarded as mad. The art of admitting to the mind only what it is capable of absorbing has been brought to perfection in the course of the history of civilization and has become in itself a source of culture. This state of affairs is not always favorable to wonder and to philosophy. They aim beyond the measure of the self-evident and disintegrate it. Yet if this disintegrating shock is immediately absorbed and integrated one does not obtain the movement that is philosophy. On the other hand, it, too, does not come into being without a "shock." There is thus a closed circle of self-evident facts, in which the introduction to wonder must seek some fissure or must bore some hole.

2. *General Education*

There is a list of things to consider and to relate to wonder: the contrast between knowledge and wonder, between ordinary and extraordinary, being at home and an exile, moderation and the lack of it, order and confusion, duality and the original link, the general and the particular, pausing in wonder and panic flight, thought inspired by wonder and thought in spite of wonder. The list is incomplete and arbitrary but it makes little difference where we begin. We are not dealing with an engine that only one procedure can start, but with a movement involving the whole of man's thought. This may be initiated at any sensitive point.

We must emphasize again that knowledge of philosophy does not make a man a philosopher, any more than knowledge of poetry makes a man a poet. He may be removed from philosophy even further than the critic is from art. Poetry written by poetry connoisseurs might show good taste, but lack inspiration and inner compulsion. The connoisseur is sometimes frustrated in his enjoyment. He is bound by tenets of good taste which prevent him from being creative. In the same way, a knowledge of everything that has been said by philosophers—which probably amounts to just about everything that can be said—might well paralyze philosophical creativity. As far as poetry and philosophy are concerned, the connoisseur is in fact nothing but a nuisance; he criticizes instead of enjoying, and talks instead of acting.

Philosophy is done rather than known. As long as doing and practicing are going on, there is as yet no true philosophy, merely a collection of philosophical sediments which are the object of philosophical knowledge. An introduction to philosophy is not a display of this collection, even if we call it "basic concepts of philosophy." There are still no philosophy, no basis, and no concepts. There is an abyss and there is wonder; there are things that make us think. The title "basic concepts of philosophy" presupposes an entire edifice, erected long ago on a solid foundation. All one needs to do is visit it and obtain information concerning those foundations and manner of construction. Then anyone, if need be, could also erect a similar building; it would be within anyone's capacity.

The phrase "basic concepts of philosophy," without the slightest irony intended, reminds one of a construction set with handbook for do-it-yourself addicts. This leads not to philosophy but at best to general education, and, in the name of philosophy, whatever it may be, we must resist it at all costs. For general education, in the sense of knowing a great deal about a great many things, is just about the exact opposite of philosophy. It is the worst and most obstinate form of knowledge and what is self-evident, while philosophy is the best and most obstinate form of ignorance and wonder.

It is the aim of philosophy to defer knowledge as long as possible, and it lives by the grace of this deferment. General education wants to know immediately, no matter how; and all it wants is to know, to get results. It is not interested in the way these results are achieved. It presupposes the absence of any form of wonder or even of curiosity. Its motives lie outside things and outside the subject. They are handed on in splended isolation by a social code in which, by an interesting process, knowledge has somehow become power and thus influence and prestige. An introduction to wonder should aim not at promoting this attitude but at criticizing it and rendering it impossible. Even if one argues that general education broadens the mind, even if one gives it an imposing Latin name like *Studium Generale*, no matter how well this course is organized it means little as an introduction or exhortation to a philosophical attitude of mind. For that is not its aim. It might well be that not everything so carefully organized and so clearly provided with goals is of real significance, that in our culture things grow more absurd in proportion to the amount of organization and institutionalization to which they are subjected. In this case wonder, which conduces to thought, may also be experienced as a feeling of unease.

General education means nothing, and this is putting it mildly. More clearly stated, we should have to say that not only has general education no positive significance—it is an enormous negative force. For general education is the wall that bolsters up mediocrity and shields it from attack by reality. It seals off the vicious circle of taking things for granted. It is a nicely rounded bubble of superficial knowledge. It enables girls straight from junior high school to prattle amiably about cultural varia, about Shakespeare, and about the atom bomb. They have heard about them and thus, if need be, can join in conversation about them, which is considered important in the social intercourse of the old school. Joining in the conversation means, first and foremost, being with it. Knowledge must at all costs be subordinate to pleasant company and togetherness. And then if a girl marries an engineer or an economist, is it not a good thing for her to be able to understand him in his work? This of course is true, but we are speaking now about a different aspect of general education. We are dealing now with general education as a form of knowledge, and that is one thing it is not. It is the exact opposite, not because it is incomplete but because it is artificially tailored.

General education is based not on real interest but at best on a sort of hobbylike quasi-interest which is not concerned with things as such but rather with the social advantages that knowledge seems to bring with it. It is a kind of soother for the satisfaction of self-emancipated women. It is stuck halfway on the road to knowledge at a point where things still provide a subject of conversation for the people in the cave, of whom Plato speaks. These people are shut inside their cave and see merely the shadows of depictions of things. The person who can talk about them best is the most generally educated person in the cave. It is he who takes the greediest pleasure in all that is provisional, unreal, refusing to look any further. For him things are self-evidently as they are and the only thing necessary is to know how they are in that self-evidence. And this presents no problem.

This allegory of the cave merits a more detailed discussion, but it is already obvious here how greatly it is based on wonder and how opposed to the culture of self-evidence. And general education is such a culture, a substitute for knowledge·among people for whom that knowledge is too dangerous and too demanding. For whatever knowledge may be, and whatever its relationship to philosophy, it originates where things are. It drags the cave dweller from the twilight of his shadow-world and hauls him outside into the pitiless light. What this comparison implies about the painfulness of the way toward actual things is important in that it sheds light on the wretchedness of general education as a screen against wonder. This education takes place at the babbling level of life in the cave or, as Heidegger would put it, in the *Gerede* of the "Man," at the level of an unreal, untried existence. It is not the product of that existence but the producer. It creates and preserves mediocrity. It does not demand that contact with things, the piercing of man's self-righteous subjectivity which is precisely the beginning of knowledge.

General education is not merely innocuous but negative in that it stifles the very existence of knowledge. This it does by sanctioning in a facile and quasi-definitive manner a knowledge that is not even worthy to be called casual acquaintance. At best it displays mountain peaks, but saves one the trouble of climbing them; it even cuts off the approaches. The person who has received a general education is familiar with some of the findings of science, but science remains for him a dark force and he is not interested in how its results were obtained. Things for him are identical with themselves, without any movement or dialectic. They are what they are and that is that. He is not conscious of any sense of wonder or loathing. At best he shows a cultured interest in lectures with lantern slides. This interest is to the fascination of the devotee as alms to social law: it does nothing to combat ignorance and even helps to preserve it.

I should be very chary of acquitting education of all responsibility for this state of affairs. The great temptation of education is to insist that one should memorize the results of science instead of flinging open its sources. This is why it costs us so much trouble in later life to delve deeper into what we have learned in a bookish and thus apodictic, authoritarian, and quasi-definitive manner. All too often at school the curiosity that might lead to closer acquaintance is nipped in the bud, and we are left with a collection of slogans and quotations that we call general education. This then is our portion of the fuss and bother they call science and, having lived through it, we can go on to other things. We have "had" it at school, but we have not got it, it has not got us, and we will never get it. Unless some intellectual crisis intervenes we are, after such a schooling, condemned to lifelong mediocrity.

One wonders indeed whether something so regularly achieved by institutional activity must not be viewed, in the long run, as its real goal. This goal might be defined as the provision of willing cave dwellers not liable to suffer from homesickness. There is no worse basis for a really penetrating knowledge than a general education. Before every new conquest it has to be demolished again. The school sanctions, from despair maybe, the superficial and the mediocre, the lack of interest. That is why it is there. A process that, of its very nature, demands infinite progression is bogged down and smoothed over in its first phase. The so-called education that results is a safety measure, to protect the cozy life in the cave.

That cave is the image of a house where no homesickness threatens and no matter how much we expand this education, quadruple it if need be, it remains the same negative force. Nowhere does it reach a point from which one could make a breakthrough to real knowledge. For real knowledge is, qualitatively speaking, of a different kind. No gradual transition is therefore possible, naturally not, for this is precisely what general education is intended to frustrate. There is thus a qualitative difference between people who have a real knowledge of anything at all and people who have had a general education, no matter how broad in scope.

3. Specialization

The connoisseur can scarcely talk to the generally educated person, for he has access at least to one thing while the other is barred from everything. The latter's talk is confined to conversation, an articulated, acoustic expression of togetherness which has no connection with actual things. There is one plain fact of experience that seems to contradict what we have just said about connoisseurs. We said that connoisseurs can be annoying and uncreative people. This assertion must be confined to a limited sort of connoisseur and knowledge, knowledge that is completely dependent on a creative culture, created by others. In company the wine connoisseur proves a hindrance to the enjoyment of a glass of wine. His expert knowledge creates an infinite number of possibilities for criticism. If the wine is not perfect, it is at once declared worthless; if it is perfect, it has to be enjoyed in the correct, minutely prescribed manner. The connoisseur creates obligations that not everyone can meet. We fear that he may be beyond a certain state of wonder and gratitude and merely makes demands. He can confine himself to stating that things are so. In this sense a connoisseur of philosophy is not yet a philosopher. Indeed he is rather an antiphilosopher since he puts a brake on wonder.

Yet there is another way of looking at the connoisseur which seems just the opposite. I should like to put it this way. In a down-to-earth conversation, that is, a conversation about actual things, the best partner on all subjects is a connoisseur on any subject, no matter what. This is increasingly true to the degree this person's knowledge is less pretentious and more specialized, more concerned with concrete things with regard to which a creative approach is important. The wine connoisseur who is a positive bore as a table companion may surprise us on other occasions with magnificent expressions derived from his speciality but which appear to have a much wider application. Anyone who has immersed himself in a certain subject is infinitely more alive to other things than the person who has stopped short at a general education, even though these subjects be completely outside his special field. This is a remarkable phenomenon which seems absolutely in conflict with the usual views on specialization and general education. The study object of our choice always appears to be much richer than when we chose it. This is essential in scientific study and the development of any kind of expertise.

General education is not necessary to provide a universal counterbalance to one-sided specialization. In this regard there are a number of current definitions that in my opinion are completely false. It is not true that the specialist is someone who knows more and more about less and less so that in the end he knows almost everything about practically nothing. He is someone who in a definite and ever more clearly defined manner has a grasp of reality in which he discovers the entire world. The danger attached to his one-sidedness exists only in the eyes of people who remain

behind among the shadows in the cave, not for the specialist himself. The purer it is, the more universal his specialized
knowledge, and of itself it requires absolutely no touching-
up, supplementing or counterbalancing by another speciality
or by philosophy. His knowledge is the prototype of true
knowledge.

In nearly all his dialogues Plato used the example of the
technicus, the skilled laborer, usually a tradesman, to illustrate what he meant by the true expert. Expertise pene-
trates to the heart of things and proceeds out from there.
The genitive *ex* is not there by accident. Like the same
case in the Latin *peritus* and its Greek equivalent, it indicates an intimate bond between knowledge and the thing.
In a certain sense the knowledge constitutes the thing and
gives it its place. This is no arbitrary subjective gesture but
an act of obedience to matter. Things that belong together
hear each other and listen to each other. Simply to accept
the pure existence of things in their uniqueness demands
an infinite sacrifice, a painful progress toward something
that is completely different, different from me and different
from what I thought it was, something thus that makes demands.

The specialist is he who follows this progress to its utmost limit; he is absorbed in his object. For him that object
is a world, not because he has projected a world into it but
for precisely the opposite reasons. He has withdrawn all his
projections, thereby allowing the object to reveal its unique
qualities. This fact emerges clearly from Gaston Bachelard's
study of the history of the natural sciences. Knowledge and
specialized knowledge are identical. If knowledge is universal it is so as specialized knowledge, and knowledge is
specialized since it attains its object at the place where it is,
not in a reflection on the thing but in the thing itself. Reflection circles round the thing, bypasses it, and returns to
the subject. Its object is knowledge of the thing rather than
the thing itself.

Reflection is a knowledge of knowing and the knower in
which the "I" curls into a question mark. It determines the

place of what Vroman calls the "curly I," the place of the individual, not the nature of the thing. It is, no matter how necessary in science and the use of labor, not a creative approach to reality, precisely because it is of its very nature a return to the subject. It confers prestige upon a variety of sciences, on intellectual criticism, methodology, planning, office work for thousands, and brief cases full of folders. It determines a large part of what is called intellectual work and is consequently important for knowledge, but it is precisely in its creative flowering that knowledge is more preoccupied with its object than with its own foundations. It owes its fascination to things, not to reflection. I can thus only determine the place of the science I practice if I indeed practice it and on the basis of that actual science. No definition can be offered beforehand or from the outside, not even by a philosophy which exhausts itself didactically and denies its true nature.

The philosophy that the specialist needs is the product of his speciality once it has gained maturity. It originates at the moment when he sees the identity of his object explode before his wondering gaze. Any other philosophy remains an unintegrated hobby, a foreign body in the study, or at best a peculiar sort of nostalgia for broader horizons that do not in fact exist. Each specialized field has its own philosophy which coincides with it. Specialization is the only form of universal knowledge. Any other sort of knowledge is a chunk of general education, cutting off access to reality. Specialized knowledge alone possesses a universal character since it lays bare reality in an authentic manner.

To say that specialized knowledge has a universal character and thus does not need to be supplemented by a more comprehensive knowledge may sound a bit paradoxical. This thesis, though, does not exclude the possibility that this knowledge might need to be supplemented. It merely stipulates that any supplementing should be knowledge. It means that the better I get to know anything at all, the more universal becomes its significance. It does not simply become more universal for me because I am naive enough to project an entire world into my special field. Naturally this does sometimes happen with enthusiastic specialists and, if we must become the dupes of the world, naivete is perhaps the best way to cushion the blow. Yet the fact remains that the wine connoisseur, who is always talking about wine, associates everything with wine, and expresses everything in wine terms, is not simply a naive sort of chap blind to everything but wine. It may be that he does indeed see a great deal through this one, trained eye, and it is surprising how many shades of feeling can be expressed with wine terms. There is more in it than you think; it is an entire world.

In the first place, the universal significance of specialized knowledge is connected with the fact that no single object is detached from a world, so that knowledge of it embraces this entire world. Second, every reality has an infinite meaning and must be the realization of an infinite number of consistent possibilities that are in principle undefinable. As knowledge increases, more possibilities are revealed. Knowledge is the discovery of the many in the one, the special thing. Its only limit is universality. Special is equivalent to universal. As applied to knowledge, the expression "one-sided specialization" is an outsider's term, good enough for the generally educated who know a lot but are overwhelmed by nothing.

The first effect of knowledge is that the special explodes and becomes universal. The basic principle of all knowledge is that the thing known is not simply the known thing, that things are not what they are and originally seemed to be, not even what they shall appear to be. The being of things is inexhaustible. This inexhaustible quality is their very being with which the "this is so" explored by knowledge can never coincide. Being is the infinitely deferred end term of knowledge and knowledge can therefore approach being only provisionally and without pretensions.

Infinite progression is possible in every form of knowledge and this progression is kept in motion by an incurable wonder that things should be different, always and in principle different. This is why we can say that we become more conscious of our ignorance the more we study. This is understandable and reasonable. Knowledge convinces us that things are different, and while this conviction is not yet knowledge, it still defines the obstinacy of wonder. When this obstinacy is cultivated we get philosophy. When the "differentness" of things is examined and noted as accurately as possible, we have specialized knowledge.

Each special field thus has its own philosophy. The wine connoisseur undoubtedly has his. For him wine is not wine or, at least, wine and wine are two different things. To a physicist iron means something different than to the generally educated person for whom it is iron and nothing more, immovably nailed to its own identity. For the classical scholar Homer is not just Homer, but not because Homer may never have existed or because his work is perhaps not his. These are merely historical details, externals. Homer is important to the classical scholar because his work reveals infinitely more to him than to anyone else. This "more" is not to be interpreted quantitatively, for it is inexhaustible.

It is thus fruitless to approach this inexhaustible quality in quantitative terms. It can only be the object of contemplation, not calculation. To the psychologist a dream is something quite different and much more than to the naive dreamer guilelessly recounting it. To the shoemaker a shoe is not just a shoe, and for the historian the same shoe has quite another manner of nonidentity since it is the tentative product of a capricious evolution, witness to its remnants and its possibilities. The craftsman, the cultural historian, or even the etymologist could find things to say about a simple shoe that would make the unbiased hearer glow with wonder or enthusiasm.

There is a trivial and self-evident identity that might be defined tautologically as: iron is iron, wine is wine, and a chair is a chair. There exists perhaps an exalted, almost divine identity that might be established through perfect knowledge. But knowledge as movement takes place in the space between; it opens things onto a world. True knowledge is universal, no matter what its object. And it is made possible by specialization, by approaching a particular piece of reality. This implies, too, that it is an authentic experience. Long before it is useful, knowledge consists in being fascinated by a piece of reality. Anyone who studies with the aim of obtaining a reasonably paid job in the labor market has a fairly reasonable chance of success, but he is far from the source of knowledge. Anyone wanting to brush up or otherwise enhance his general education is just as far away. They remain forever imprisoned in the cave. Knowledge is a disinterested matter.

This sounds like an arguable statement, in keeping with a bygone alien philosophy. But we could also put it this way: knowledge in itself is always more fascinating than its most useful and most salutary object; or even: knowledge is autonomous, like art. Knowledge and art are autonomous, but not the connoisseur and the artist. Knowledge makes inexorable demands. Authentic experience of reality is the first of these but it is not one that can be met arbitrarily and with any amount of effort. The experience we are talking about is felt as a shock, the *expérience-choc* which Thévenaz regards as the principle of rational mobility. It is the foundation of wonder and knowledge. It is the sledgehammer that pulverizes our self-righteousness and opens the world to us. And it matters little where this happens. An elaboration on all other points is possible from any point since true wonder is universal. Once mobilized, the choice of object is of little importance. To someone with an open mind it makes little difference whether he studies mathematics or literature. Nor is he in any danger of exhausting the object of his wonder. We might provisionally define wonder as the contemplation of a concrete infinity, but we shall have to elaborate on this definition.

Two

WONDER AND PHILOSOPHY

1. Wonder and Openness

What we call wonder is not one clearly definable feeling but a range of possibilities. Even the word "feeling," vague as it is, is still too sentimental a definition. We might do better to speak of "disposition" in the sense of self-experience in a particular situation. In wonder we experience ourselves on the basis of a confrontation with a reality. Wonder admits of a range of possibilities since it is an experience of self on the way to and groping for an attitude with regard to the reality with which we are confronted. It is not yet an attitude or a feeling but the concentration from which an attitude or a feeling may possibly develop. To become angry or to give way to sorrow is to determine already our feeling and our attitude. But before becoming angry or shy or enthusiastic I must, as it were, take mental stock of the situation.

Wonder is a disposition which has not yet identified itself as a particular and orientated feeling. It thus changes character as it changes direction. It possesses this range of possibilities before this choice precisely as wonder which has not yet chosen a way out. Wonder can shade from slight, by way of surprise, astonishment and amazement right up to dismay and horror. The degree is determined by the nature of the person and of the situation. What one finds surprising, the other may find self-evident. One may certainly speak of a talent for wonder. In a more philosophizing or philosophic sense of the word, wonder is the experience of self between establishing that a reality is thus and that it is different, the melting point between liquidity or evaporation and opacity or petrifaction. Confronting reality at this point it is the state of suspension between the grasped and the ungrasped. It is one and the other or neither one nor the other, never one without the other.

Wonder is a certainty which has only just been established and has not yet lost the expectation of seeing its opposite appear. This does not exclude the knowledge of that which is incited by wonder. On the contrary: the more we know about something the more clearly we realize that this knowledge is never exhaustive. Knowledge may nourish wonder since it can postulate the possibility that things may be different than they are. I should not wonder at the sun's rising if I were not convinced of the possibility that some day it might not. Only those things that nobody thinks about are self-evident. Wonder that a thing is so is motivated by the possibility that it might be different. This movement is endless since this "difference" remains completely undefined. Wonder and the idea of "the other" are of vital importance in the impulse to philosophize, but these are not philosophical terms or principles—rather the contrary. They indicate a shock, a happening, impossible to integrate in an existing system and around which no new system can ever grow up.

Wonder is not without danger; it is capable of disintegrating an existence. This may explain why wonder is a theme about which much is said but also a phenomenon to which few devote themselves in order to find a new impulse for life and thought. People prefer to strip wonder of

its dangerous aspects. It is frequently viewed rather roman-
tically. The idea of wonder conjures up a certain type of
poet, existing only in the imagination, who proceeds
through life in a wide-eyed, childish fashion, always wondering at things that others do not see or else find completely ordinary. This is more a sort of immaturity or lack
of realism than true contact with reality. People prefer to
forget that wonder can intensify this contact and be a painful pathos. Yet there is a grain of truth in this romantic or
quasi-romantic picture; wonder is completely disinterested.
Its interest is deferred to the infinite; it is not directly concerned with the incarnation. This it has in common with
all that is great and spiritual, which probably explains why
people are somewhat embarrassed by it.

Wonder belongs in the pathic, passive sector of life. It
is openness, vulnerability. A closed attitude renders it impossible, for this might be termed a spiritual grasping at
all that is directly necessary, practicable, tangible, the fear
of losing what one regards as reality but what is in fact a
product of one's own arbitrariness. This disposition, as it
were, banishes the spirit from things and reduces them to
ordinariness. Wonder and a closed mind are mutually ex-
clusive since wonder prevents the development of a closed
circle, a system. It is the very principle of openness. It is
thus in the interest of the closed circle of the system, including the scientific system and method, to banish the disinterested from its domain.

To introduce someone to wonder, to plunge someone
into wonder is thus in a certain sense an aggressive act
insofar as it necessitates breaking open this closed circle.
We deliberately say, *plunge into wonder*, for wonder, like
enthusiasm or inspiration, is something that cannot be artificially aroused or imitated. It is something that happens
to people. It is an adventure whose outcome one cannot
foresee, an exercise in free fall, and as an adventure it is a
prelude to an open and disinterested attitude to life. Wonder situates man outside his world and happens to him
from the world outside his world. It happens to him as a
natural phenomenon and can thus rightly be called disin-

terested. But anyone once exposed to it cannot shake off the effects.

What happens to man when he wonders? His open mind reveals a world to him that until then had been closed. Wondering is staring into a world which until recently was a different world and now proves to be his own, or vice versa. It is usually said to originate from the contrast between the usual and the unusual. It can happen to us when the unusual appears to be usual, explicable, and comprehensible but equally so when the usual reveals itself as unusual or shows an unusual side. This seesawing is caused not only by the ambivalent character of wonder but by the dubious value of the notions "usual" and "unusual." For we do not know what is usual so long as the unusual has not become relevant. The significance of usual and unusual only springs from the contrast. So long as there is no question, in a closed existence, of the unusual or different, the usual is not implicitly present as such and wonder can only exist at best in a very degraded form, as the impulse to remove that which threatens to become unusual. The word here should really be "banal." The banal is the usual which has not yet been exposed to the crisis of confrontation with its opposite. Without this crisis there is no wonder.

Wonder is a crisis and has all the dangers inherent in a crisis. A crisis exists when a person is forced to review the structure of his existence and break out of his closed circle into a greater openness. This is why wonder and the notions of usual and unusual are to a certain extent subjective and relative. What might be unusual to one may be quite usual to the other. For, to a certain degree, depending on how susceptible we are to wonder, we can become used to the unusual. Not everyone wonders at the same thing, since the extent of our wonder is determined among other things by the acquisitions of our individual existence. The permanent and substantial elements in wonder are openness and crisis. Since wonder overcomes us as a crisis it is not the milk-and-watery, childish thing it appears to the banal thinker.

The very fact that wonder happens to us makes it a

form of suffering. Everything that happens to man despite himself is suffering, regardless of what form it takes, for this merely determines whether this happening is experienced as suffering or not. In this sense even the graces and favors accorded to man are a suffering, a pathos, and people who in their self-righteousness are active by nature will find this passive character hard to accept. They are indeed suffering from a favor. Wonder also means suffering and danger since it plunges man from his closed world into an open one, from self-interest into disinterest, and thus compels him to integrate his life anew.

2. *Wonder as a Principle*

Wonder puts man at the mercy of things. In the first place he wonders about things, not himself. Wonder gives things their meaning. Wonder shows them to be significant. It is a step nearer the realization that things have an infinite meaning and that this meaning is attributable to the things themselves and not to man and his interests. It can free him from a tenacious self-righteousness and give his existence a new dimension. This dimension might loosely be termed "disinterestedness" but might also be pleasure, enjoyment, enthusiasm, or meditation. This new insight is extremely fundamental. It means that in wonder things do not exist for man, man exists for things. He exists to contemplate things, to possess them and to wonder at them. "Zum Erstaunen bin ich da," says Goethe. Man cannot exhaust the meaning of things by incorporating them in the sphere of his interests or by using them, not even those things he has made himself and may thus, with some justification, regard as the products of his own arbitrary power. The only possible approach to their meaning is that of disinterested contemplation. But contemplation is the attitude adopted towards the infinite. To contemplate things in wonder is to attribute to them an infinite significance. This is why it is the only adequate attitude.

Wonder signifies, therefore, the beginning of contemplation. But what is the beginning of something endless other than its totality? If the beginning cannot be contrasted with an end, it is itself the decisive and radical step into infinity. The word "beginning" here recalls Aristotle's statement that man has always arrived at philosophy through wonder, in former times and still today. It is thus not something that happens once and for all with a permanent result and a lasting, visible effect. Philosophizing, with every philosopher, always begins and ends with wonder. Plato states this even more decisively when he says that there is no other *archè*, no other beginning or principle of philosophy than the pathos of wonder. "For wonder is the feeling of a philosopher and philosophy begins in wonder."

Plato makes Socrates say this, and it sounds in this passage a trifle ironical. Yet Socrates' irony is also a way of saying startling things. And what he has to say here is radical in the extreme: he decisively excludes any other principle of philosophy. It is all the more surprising thus that this statement receives only a passing mention in all sorts of philosophical works. It is often quoted to round off the chapter on wonder while the author then carries on without giving any sign of wonder at all. Is there any philosopher at all whose thoughts and writings proceed directly and honestly from wonder and the fascination of things without the detour of a method and without sophistry? And would such a philosopher be accepted? Would he not be called the dupe of a danger that is also inherent in wonder?

Even in Plato and Aristotle there is little trace, at first glance, of wonder as the primary principle of their thought. And yet they do not "merely" call wonder the beginning of philosophy. The word *archè* employed by Plato indicates something other than a beginning. It is not an *initium* but a *principium*. Thomas Aquinas uses the same word when he calls wonder the principle of philosophy. The wonder he refers to, as Pieper says, not only is the beginning of all philosophy in the sense of *initium*, first stage or first step, but is the principle or inner abiding cause of all philosophizing. Should it be absent, then philosophizing would degenerate into ideology or science. Heidegger has pointed out that *archè* is derived from a verb which means "to bring forward," "to lead."

Philosophy allows itself to be lead by wonder which in turn leads the philosopher to the true attitude toward being. Even at that, "to lead" is perhaps too weak a word for what this principle does. It does not lead along a long road toward something completely different and very far away. Wonder is the foundation of the whole of philosophy. It is not the beginning of thought in the sense that it might lead on to something better founded, something like philosophical principles, which could be cheerfully manipulated without any ambiguity. Nor does the philosopher begin by wondering, proceed to an examination, and thus rid himself of a tiresome guest. It is not the beginning but the principle, the basic structure. It is not only the beginning but also the end; it guides and accompanies thought. It has not only the first but also the last word. The philosopher does not get over it, like a childish disease, but ascends to it with difficulty as the only adequate attitude toward the mystery of things. It is the principle that determines the infinity of contemplation. It does not, therefore, precede all knowledge as a power-motivating curiosity, but may just as well be a product of knowledge. It is precisely the realization that things are as they are, the provisional end term of an acquaintance with things, that moves wonder to contemplation.

Wonder then, according to these texts of Plato and Aristotle, must be viewed as the core of all philosophical thought; it determines its philosophical quality. Yet the fact remains that there is not a single philosopher who demonstrably allows himself to be guided by the pathos of wonder. He is guided by logic, by methods, by principles, but not by wonder. In some way or another wonder still seems to be something the philosopher must surmount without feeling himself a sophist. It is equally certain, however, that it cannot be viewed as a provisional or deficient method. It

is even more than a point of departure and more fundamental than a methodical doubting.

Doubt may accompany wonder for a moment, the moment at which the closed circle is pierced. But more happens in wonder than in doubt. Perspectives immediately
open or may even be already there when wonder acts.
Doubt is associated with a logical series of thoughts which
must be coherent. This already presumes more than wonder
did; thought has already established itself as a form of
reasoning. Instead of wonder as a principle of contemplation we have logic as a way of reasoning. Doubt is thus
less fundamental than wonder. It originates on a different
level where there is already a clear choice between different
modes of thought. This may be why, in the history of
philosophy, doubt is taken much more seriously than wonder. It is closer to the scientific pretensions that philosophy
has acquired.

Perhaps the wonder of which the philosophers speak is
not real wonder but another name for what might be better
termed "question." Is it a doubt, a wondering, or a question
when Heidegger, as the point of departure of metaphysical
thought, poses the "question": "Warum ist uberhaupt Sie-
endes und nicht vielmehr nichts?" This question certainly
proceeds from wonder, but is it also a direct expression of
wonder? Has wonder here not already been transformed
into a question? If wonder could express itself directly, would
it be as great certainty or as a question? If wonder is
indeed a not yet identified disposition, it is not adequately
expressed either in a question or in a positive affirmation.
Question and doubt are already manipulations of the material afforded by wonder, curved in the direction of reasoning and answer, series and system. The "why" of the question
"Why does something exist?" is already clearly twisted in
the direction of a category like causality and implies the
expectation of a particular sort of answer. It is already
evident that it is a game with constituted basic principles
and cannot thus be fundamental. Wonder here is too hasty
in seeking an outlet to be a principle. The affirmation

"There is something and there might also be nothing" would already be more fundamental, but even this would not be the same thing as wonder.

The principle remains silent in the background. It cannot be directly formulated, not in the question which requires an answer nor in the affirmation—not even should the actual question, detached from the categories of a constituted philosophy, be posed as an affirmation without engagement: "It is strange that there is something and not nothing." It may be that wonder is not at all practicable as the first and sole principle of philosophy. But this would not be reason for making it artificially practicable, but rather for limiting philosophy to what is given with wonder.

Now the step from wonder to question is fairly small, and the Greek verb used by Plato and Aristotle for "to wonder" can also be translated as "to ask oneself wonderingly." This is a very common meaning. It must thus be said that wonder and question, though indicated by the same word, are not the same thing. The question is already seeking an outlet for wonder; it has already absorbed a piece of wonder. This may perhaps explain why philosophy is so willing to preach wonder as its principle and so reluctant to practice it. It tries to get over wonder, not as an illness but as something impossible to work with. From time immemorial philosophy has been an attempt to arrive at science, and this may well be its besetting sin. Should philosophy not confine itself to expressing wonder? This is where the difficulty lies. Wonder cannot be expressed without question or affirmation and this question or affirmation opens the series that leads away from wonder toward science. Admittedly science in its turn provokes wonder, but this too is assimilated again. In this way it is degraded and becomes, as it were, the waste product of a thought process, the aim of which is increasingly scientific. It is possible to imagine a philosophy whose only concern is to gather itself up from anywhere and glean its bits and pieces from the ecstasy of wonder and amazement, and leave all the rest to science.

As we have already said, a distinction must be made between a trivial and a divine identity. To knowledge, things are not identical. The wonder aroused at first acquaintance, when it discovers that a thing is so, also discovers the possibility that it might be different. Wonder as a thesis might be framed: Nothing is just as it is, everything is different. Reflection upon wonder also subjects this thesis to its own rule. Wonder is not identical with itself. Affirmation and question both have places within its restive identity. If wonder is the principle of philosophy, it can also be the anti-principle. The same wonder may inspire the contemplative pause and reasoning continuation, ecstacy and agitation. The relationship between philosophy and science, between philosophy as observation and philosophy as a system or construction, is contained within the same restive identity of wonder.

Precisely because philosophy can never get over wonder it is eternally tempted to ignore it completely. Even earlier than Plato's statement that wonder is the beginning of all philosophy we have Democritus' stand against wonder. It was he who said, "Imperturbable wisdom is invaluable." Better known still is the Stoic *nil admirari*. Resistance to wonder which evidently springs from a deep philosophical instinct is older than Stoicism and can thus hardly be attributed to the Stoic mentality which disapproves of emotions such as wonder. Nor is there any evidence that each case concerns a different sort of wonder—in Plato and Aristotle, for instance, an inquiring curiosity and in Democritus an inner pang. We might try to argue that the positive appreciation of wonder by Plato and Aristotle is linked with their more contemplative concept of philosophy, while Democritus and the Stoics try to master it because they are more scientifically oriented, but this thesis would be hard to prove.

We would do better to ascribe these contradictions to the tensions existing within the identity of wonder itself which cannot be automatically aroused or artificially continued. This being so, we can scarcely deny that philosophy is an enemy of wonder. Wonder admittedly gives philosophy its prestige, and guides it, pointing out the way to things in their infinity, but from the outset there is a philosophy that is not content with this. Besides wonder, passivity, it also desires work, activity, realization in some branch of learning. This being so it must absorb and surmount wonder. As Bachelard strikingly puts it: "Il faut digérer la surprise." But this implies intense preoccupation. Philosophy is this preoccupation, and the *nil admirari* of the Stoics is for philosophy an unattainable ideal which above all must not be considered a rule of conduct. It merely means that wonder, even as a principle, remains ineffable, and thus, given the eloquence of philosophy, remains the "other," a foreign body within its own identity. Wonder prevents philosophy from constituting, establishing itself.

3. *The Physiognomy of Wonder*

Wonder brings a moment of pause to thought. We say that a person "halts in amazement." This is significant. This halting is a cessation of movement, planning, intervening. The expression "to halt in amazement" presumes thus an active life that is suddenly interrupted and pulled up short. Wonder is situated in the middle of a movement. Before and after wonder there is movement which is the "normal" state. People, it would seem, are primarily movers and workers. To halt is also to cease talking; the "differentness" of things reveals itself in the silence. One must listen in order to catch it, and be careful lest one drowns it out as with every revelation. The event of wonder does not occur without a minimum of attention.

To halt is also to stand up straight, to watch intently for the apparition of the other. It means being ready to integrate as quickly as possible whatever strange thing may occur and thus to absorb wonder. With all this it is a being open to observe whatever happens, being totally receptive. For wonder is openness. Yet halting in wonder is not a purposeful action, but rather a disinterested act of expression, an expression of the encounter in which man also meets himself. Maximum openness gives maximum self-experience. Halting however is not the fact of being concentrated but the very act of concentration. The person who halts in wonder collects himself and ranges himself against the world. Impelled by the shock of amazement he comes to himself, gathers himself together from the diaspora of bewilderment.

"Standing" is an immanent, panic occupation within one's own identity in order to be able to insert one's identity into the situation; it is not a permanent situation but an ongoing process of coming-to-a-stop, of standing still, of standing fast, summoning one's own substantiality to hope in order to resist what is happening. This halting is the human way of being present in the midst of things. In this way the whole human body, from head to toe, can experience and express the fact of wonder. This expressing is not an arbitrary availing of the means of expression given to man; he experiences what he expresses rather than expressing what he is experiencing. This halting does not result from an inner deliberation; it is the involuntary break in a rhythm not only of thought but of the whole of life.

Wonder is a vital experience even though the person who halts, falls out of line, sinks into contemplation, and remains behind may seem to become peculiar and barren. In wonder it is not only the intelligence that capitulates before the complicatedness of things but the whole of life that crumbles before an obstacle. Thought is not a faculty divorced from that life but life itself in its most complicated form. Thought only acquires its own independence through a long-drawn-out process in which wonder is radicalized. This is why wonder may be expressed in the totality of the human appearance, even in the breath and the circulation of the blood. When we halt in wonder we say that we hold our breath, but we might equally say that the breath catches in our throat. We may also listen in breathless wonder to a fascinating lecture or a piece of music. Our rhythm of life ceases for a moment in order to concentrate on keeping time with a different rhythm. This is the significance of the physiognomical expression of wonder. It is the attitude of someone temporarily shaken out of his shell or even of a mentally backward person.

The effect of wonder is never so clear as on those who are less gifted intellectually. They are entirely overwhelmed by things. They see that they are there, in great quantities, but the connection is not clear to them. Knowledge that is limited to things as they are, to a simple observation of the fact that they are so—without any suspicion that they might be different but also without the capacity to confirm them in their identity—can lead to a helpless, total wonder which can be expressed only by the wide-open mouth. It is a sign of total and unconditional capitulation. Anyone who views the world thus renounces any attempt to create order in it. He would not know where to begin. He is completely passive in the face of events but very interested.

In a further phase we see the eyebrows raised. This is a less unconditional form of capitulation. It expresses a vague suspicion that order might be established in that chaos. It might even be interpreted as a frozen impulse to begin on this task. In order to complete the picture we might interpret the vertical frown as an expression of aggression and the beginnings of assimilation while the horizontal wrinkle expresses only acceptance. Any wonder that remains completely devoid of this impulse to assimilate must of necessity remain philosophically unfruitful since it stagnates, as it were, in its own identity.

To sum up, with Buytendijk: "Wonder is characterized by a halting of the thing observed. This halting, which men call attention, is at the same time permeated by a premonition that light may be shed on this thing. Whatever is new and arouses wonder must have some known features, must presume a certain familiarity." This assumption is its salvation. Without this perspective wonder degenerates into helpless bewilderment. In this respect it is instructive to compare the wondering face of the young Holderlin vith that of his old age and madness. As Picard says, the fire, which he received from heaven into his own hands, struck this starry face like lightning, causing it to disintegrate completely. Wonder must be assimilated if it is not to be fatal.

4. Wonder and Fascination

There is a constant dialectic in progress between pure wonder and its assimilation in reasoning and systems. Philosophical thought takes place within this dialectic. It is life and self-preservation. Wonder may well be to philosophy what inspiration is to poetry. It is indeed the essential thing but even when this essential thing is present the work that we call philosophy or poetry is only just beginning. Inspiration cannot take the place of work; wonder cannot usurp the place of the craftsmanlike thought of which Heidegger speaks. The philosopher cannot speak directly from fascination. Not even the poet can do this, still less those whose work lies in the positive sciences. The craft of science is to a large extent sundered from philosophy and thus, as work, even further removed from fascination. And yet it would certainly be a commendable thing if both gave clearer evidence of their wonder and fascination which remain the source and origin of their craft, no matter how exactly and methodically they may attempt to carry it out.

Wonder is only a danger insofar as the perspectives that it affords are presented in a chaotic manner. It is only dangerous thus to those who try to bring order into this chaos, not for those who can accept it as it is or who leave the ordering to others. They may not be philosophers in the fairly pretentious meaning this word has acquired after its modest origins but their attitude is not unconnected with wisdom and contemplation. The revelation of the chaos that exists beyond the closed and regulated world has a fascinating effect for the contemplative person. Chaos menaces man only insofar as he is afraid. Wonder is a danger to the fearful. It may well be that fear is the greatest enemy of wonder, which may explain why it is also the greatest and most fanatical champion of clear-cut method in life and thought. Viewed in this light, method is a means of averting chaos, fear of a direct experience of reality.

Augustine has something rather marvelous to say about wonder. He says that it strikes the heart without hurting it (*Percutit cor meum sine laesione*). The heart longs for the new that is revealed in wonder "inasmuch as it is like it," and recoils from it inasmuch as it is unlike it. Here again we meet the dialectic between the usual and unusual which gives wonder its prestige. This wonder is not really sufficient to sustain philosophy and we can therefore continue to ask ourselves, despite the assurances of Plato and Aristotle, whether pure wonder is indeed a philosophical attitude, whether there is not a degree of openness, contemplation, or passivity that expresses wonder more adequately than does classical philosophy.

It is clear that Greek philosophy originated from wonder, but this appears to be something quite different from the attitude suggested by a watered-down poetism. It consists in being fascinated by the reality of things. This fascination inspired the thoughts and utterances of the pre-Socratics who were originally without method and somewhat dilettantic, as the name "philosopher" suggests. From this starting point they developed into philosophers. This required skilled thinking and specialization.

Not everyone who wonders is a philosopher; this wonder must be radicalized. Without this radicalization it is not worth surmounting. In the trade of thinking an attempt is made to assimilate wonder and to contain chaos. This is the philosopher's resistance to wonder. It is clear from this that wonder as a purely passive attitude, allowing oneself to be overwhelmed, is not the philosophical attitude par excellence it is often taken to be. The philosopher proceeds from wonder to his craft of thinking. This "from" signifies distance; he does not philosophize toward wonder but away from it. Wonder is not a goal but an obstacle. The sense of being overwhelmed finds its counterpart in the force of autonomous thought.

The philosopher emancipates himself from the fascination of things. Pre-Socratic philosophy is now emancipated from archaic religion and mythology. Before becoming philosphers, the pre-Socratics were classical religious individuals. Their philosophy is detached from the classical religion. For this reason it would be more accurate to call it symbolism or natural mysticism rather than philosophy in the technical and increasingly more scientific form in which we know it today. Symbolic thinking is a manner of thought in which the fascination of things is preeminent and for that reason alone it is interesting.

The wonder that the pre-Socratics transformed into doubt and questioning is a religious attitude. Fascination is a religious phenomenon. Wonder is a religious element in philosophy and poetry, but one would have to be able to define the relationship between religion and philosophy, between religion and poetry, pretty exactly in order to conclude that wonder is a foreign body in philosophy. In any case, wonder is also a religious attitude. In a religion with a minimum of dogmas and elaborations of the *ganz Andere,* wonder might be able to remain itself. The dialogue between the usual and the unusual, which at first sight appeared to lie at the origin of wonder, seems here to derive its force from the much more powerful dialogue between the sacred and the profane, the Diesseits and the Jenseits, the similar and the different, or whatever one wishes to call this contrast.

Wonder itself may already be an assimilation of bewilderment, dismay, ecstasy. The religious character emerges much more clearly in these words, for that matter in the word "wonder" itself, especially when we trace it back to wonder in the sense of miracle and remember the words of Schleiermacher who said that "miracle" is the religious name for event. The wonder one wonders about is the event of the revelation of things. It is the sudden revelation of the sacred, the marvelous, originating from another world. But this other world has here not yet been made concrete in the shape of a world that really exists, in another place, at another time, and in a different manner, a world distinct from our own.

The wonder in the sense of miracle, the religious name for the unexpected, the unknown, is an incarnation of the *ganz Andere*. Wonder leaves nothing "usual." "Everything is different" is wonder's motto, but naturally it applies only to an extreme, unattainable, and unsurvivable frontier of wonder. Beneath this frontier the contrast between the usual and the unusual continues to exist and the religious experience of this contrast is a constant source of wonder. For this reason religious phenomenologists like Söderblom and Van der Leeuw call it a basic religious attitude.

The usual, completely assimilated to life, is no longer a revelation. This is why the usual, as Theophrastus says, is not a *teras*, not a cause for amazement, not a divine sign from another world. It has not the value of a revelation since it is not experienced as coming from another world; it is identical in a trivial manner. Only that which is different, or the ordinary experienced as different, is numerous, mysterious. Wonder is man's attitude in the face of the mystery of things. For this reason it is in principle powerless, nonregulating. Mystery is a key word in the religious life. As long as the mystery is in some way accepted and experienced, it is possible to feel wonder. The *nil admirari* is the end of mystery, and thus the goal of reasonable thought. Democritus and the Stoa may have insisted upon it impatiently and prematurely in order to fence off philoscphy from classical religion. By so doing they put an end to the religious nature of philosophy and signaled the beginning of a more technical-scientific way of thought. Stoicism is the first philosophy to lay claim to replace the ancient religion.

Wonder is the beginning of wisdom in the same way as is the fear of the Lord. They may, in some way or other, be identical. On the one hand wonder is perpetual disquiet. Unsuspected meanings are glimpsed in ordinary things. It constantly compels us to come out into the open, to review our world and existence. It is a crisis. Yet on the other hand it is not granted to anyone who does not already put his trust in those forces that regulate the chaos. We should not dare to be fearful, were we not sure of surviving our fear. We should not dare to sleep without the certainty of awakening. In the same way we cannot wonder without a feeling of security in a world-ground. We can only wonder, we only dare to give way to wonder, if we are confident that in wondering this world-ground will not crumble beneath our feet. Without this confidence, fearful though it may be, wonder may turn any minute into loathing or panic.

Wonder is only possible within a feeling of security, and if the feeling of security is childish we might also say that there is something childish about wonder. Or perhaps "childlike" would be more accurate. The childlike state is not a rudiment but an acquirement, perhaps the most important. And insofar as the childlike state is an acquirement, the gift of wonder can also be acquired and an introduction to wonder be meaningful.

Three

BEWILDERMENT

1. The Noonday Devil and the Siesta

We in the north can hardly be said to know the sun. To us it is the benevolent planet which gives a bit of color to our misty lives. Closer to the equator, however, the sun is the Bengal tiger which can kill as well as give life. Paying as little heed to this idea as to the scientific fact that the sun is a perpetual explosion, we have, in our light and sun symbolism, placed too much stress on the benevolent element. This has blinded us to the dangerous ambivalence attached to this symbol in archaic southern life.

Of all the cosmic hierophanics (to use an elegant phrase of Eliade's) the sun and light are the most underestimated, the victims of a short-sighted rationalism. They have been transformed into symbols of reasonableness. The rationalization consists in the fact that the symbol is deprived of its ambivalence; it is no longer a symbol but a reasonable allegory, a clear sign of reference. In this way not only the sun but reason that is symbolized by the sun has lost its demonic character. They have become unambiguous, purely positive, things with a plain and undisputed identity. The sun is no longer an explosion. Yet this also robs the symbol of its sacred character, for in the archaic sense of the word the sacred is the ambivalent, dangerous aspect which never loses its menace.

When we learn of ancient and ethnological facts concerning sun myths, rites, and cults, we arbitrarily assume that the mentality that gave rise to them resembles our own. We take it for granted that the sun is simply accepted as it is, that it is only adored, but not feared, cursed, or conjured. In order to show how incorrect such an attitude is, I should like, making as much use as possible of contemporary terminology, to discuss the symbolism of the hour of noon, summed up in the figure of the noonday devil, and its significance for thought and culture. "Devil" in this combination is in actual fact an incorrect translation of *daimon*, since it retains only an unfavorable meaning, while *daimon* is typically ambivalent and lies much more in the sphere of the sacral. The term thus is something of a hybrid. On the one hand we think of noon as a purely positive zenith which is not, as in archaic thought, at the same time a nadir and, by this ambivalence, sacral, while on the other hand we are accustomed to attribute to the devil only a negative significance as the personification of evil and opponent of the divinity.

Yet "noonday devil" is the usual translation of what the Psalmist calls, in the Vulgate, *daemon meridianus* (90:6). The demon is here numbered among the dangers against which the Lord protects his own. The new Latin translation speaks here of a *pernicies quae vastat meridie*, a "destruction that wastes at noonday." This destruction must be taken to refer to the danger of noon in general, and not especially sunstroke or something similar. I do not know whether this *daemon meridianus* of the Psalm is identical with the one I am discussing here. One thing of which I am certain is that the celebrated clerical interpretation of the *démon du midi* as the personification of the difficulties that beset celibates at about the noonday of their lives has no foundation either in the Bible or in classical thought.

This noon is in fact the middle of the day, the midday hour when the sun has reached its zenith. The noonday devil is this actual noon, but in its dangerous form. Noon is the dangerous hour of the day. This is what makes it special and susceptible to personification in the figure of a demon. As Erwin Rohde expressly observes, noon and midnight are the classic haunting hours. It is then that Empusa walks in various shapes, sowing bewilderment and alarm; these are the witching hours. At the critical moment of midday the unexpected sounds of Pan spread panic fear in a world that has fallen silent. At noon, life hesitates to recognize the sun as its origin for it is noon that menaces life with death and destruction. This may be why the Elgoinyi, an African tribe, adore the sun only as it rises and not when it has reached its zenith. Only the rising of the sun causes life to rise; standing still it is a menace to life.

There is thus a certain parallelism between midday and midnight, perfect light and absolute darkness. Both are dangerous and critical and therefore witching hours. Midday and midnight are dangerous because they are critical phases in the progress of the sun's course and of time. Round about midday and midnight the wheel of time seems to stand still for a moment or at least to hesitate. The course of the sun is no more to be taken for granted than its rise. Something might happen at any moment and noon is preeminently such a moment. During the night, day delves deep into the dark arsenal of its potentialities and uses them to create new forces. It might, however, be tempted to sink into the infinity of this ocean or, having reached its zenith, might refuse to return to the ocean. Then the rhythm of life would falter and life itself dry up.

It is at this time that primitive man feels the urge to intervene in the rhythm of the cosmos, to get it going again, to circulate the vital forces through his magic influence. His rites must influence the course of natural events and insure him against the dangers of the critical phase. These rites cause the sun to reappear from its nadir, protect man against the "destruction that wastes at noonday," or appease it with the blood of a human heart.

Midday, antipole of midnight, is the zenith of day and light and thus is light in its most ambivalent form. At noon, clarity, light, and heat become something absolute, cease to be functions, are transformed into concrete substances, and replace all other concrete substances. Midday threatens to destroy the world that was built up by the morning. In this world man loses his grip of reality; he no longer recognizes it. It acquires the demonic character of that which is entirely different and in it loses its matter-of-factness. In this paradox of light which is the southern noon, things lose the contours which only a tempering of light can give them, movements cease, and sound becomes impotent while in its place the silence becomes audible. In the absolute light, which we tend to regard as the symbol of a reasonable mind, without demons or ambiguity, nothingness grazes in an empty world. "Dann waltet die absolute Gesprächlosigkeit" (Ernesto Grassi). For all sound is deliberation; this absolute silence signifies the approach and impotent contemplation of the elements of the inexorable.

At noonday there is the danger that life may be delivered up to this absolute light and its fatal clarity, which dissolves the opacity in which life veils its substance and protects it from destruction, and to absolute heat, which burns the substance out of things, becoming substance in their place. Noon and light dissect and enervate the world. Noon sucks out its essence to where it is dissolved in the nothingness of light. Light is fatal; it robs things of their identity. Nothing can withstand it. The heat and light of noon are paralyzing. The noonday devil commands silence and halts the rhythm of life in order to impose his own. He is an occurrence which cannot be predicted or overwhelmed by the light of reason, the absolute mastery of the other.

Pan slumbers at noon by the shore of a cool stream and woe betide anyone who disturbs him! But it sometimes happens that Pan does not slumber, that his noise alarms the slumbering world. The noonday devil is also the personification of absolute light. Unlike the light of early morning it does not glide past things, playfully and respectfully, leaving them unaltered in their own obscurity. It halts unashamedly, and becoming tangible, takes the place of things. This light is no longer truth but desolation.

This absolute character of noon can acquire a metaphysical and eschatological perspective. The end symbolized here by noon is a typically eschatological end, an extremity, a zenith that is at the same time nadir and crisis. Nothing similar can follow such an end, only the beginning of a completely different existence. It is not an end in time, but in a plane of existence. It signifies the interruption of the "other" into one's arbitrary, same existence. Wonder and amazement possess this eschatological perspective in the paradoxically simultaneous fact that things are as they are and yet are completely different. The end is not an end in time but an explosion of possibilities.

Midday is the hour at which the world can lose its familiar face, can dissolve in a primeval fire in which it is revealed to the bewildered eyes of the noonday spectator as a perpetual explosion of ineffable possibilities where he imagined he saw a clearly defined reality. Vincent van Gogh, the painter of noon, ventured into this chaos of eschatological lightning flashes and was obliged to pay for his audacity with permanent bewilderment. For it is *hubris* to try to give shape to the absolute. In this hour of terror Nietzsche experiences his *groszer Mittag*. To be a match for noon is to have survived the absolute crisis, a new beginning, and guarantee of an existence in an *ewige Wiederkehr*. He who survives this *hubris* is the *Übermensch*. He lives like the phoenix which rises from its ashes or like a classical hero who gains immortality only through death.

Had not Plato just such an experience in mind when he penned the comparison with the cave? He describes in detail how much it hurts the eyes to see things in the light of the sun after having seen their shadows in the cave. No one can survive this crisis of clarity, this sight of the sun. If he does not die of this direct confrontation with the absolute which disintegrates his entire life, he will be killed by his fellow mortals in the cave who are content with the shadows of pictures of things. They do not desire to experience the terrors of the light, not even in the form of a story, since they are instinctively aware of its dangers.

Noon is the crisis of clarity just as midnight is the crisis of obscurity. Both destroy the world by reducing it to pure actuality or pure virtuality and push men out of the world. Or should we say that man himself flees from the world at these critical eschatological moments? Nowhere perhaps is the archaic parallelism of cosmic and psychic life so mysterious as here. For besides actually intervening in the course of natural events by his magic rites, man has another attitude toward the crisis which we might almost call an anti-rite, a passive rite. Is it only the *Übermensch* who reacts actively and magically, and the Platonic cave dweller who retires to the shadow to slumber until the danger is past?

Sleep might be considered such an anti-rite. The contrast between day and night is not only one of light and darkness but just as essentially one of waking and sleeping. Day is the time of waking and light, of fixed contours and acute awareness. Waking is a symbol of tension in existence, of being attuned to the clearly defined outlines and indivisible identity of things that can only be grasped in this manner. It is a state of alarm. To be awake is to be vigilant, to be on guard to guarantee the shape of things. Waking consciousness might be said to replace light and assume its task. It is itself the light that guarantees to each thing its particular form. Sleep then signifies a renouncing of this ontological vigilance, a sinking back into the amorphous darkness, hoping that even without awareness things will retain their shape. Sleep might be called realistic while waking is idealistic and renders being dependent upon thought.

Darkness, in which things lose their shape, is an invitation to sleep. Nightly sleep is a passive rite in which man confirms the parallelism between cosmic and human life by closing his eyes and withdrawing from a world that has grown amorphous. Light, however, summons us to vigilance, and the absolute light of noon is an invitation to absolute vigilance. Noon is the supreme test of idealistic awareness. It compels our conscious senses to restore to things the shape that it deprives them of in broad daylight. This is the parallelism in danger for all who witness the noonday crisis. But is this not a superhuman task? So it would appear. Is this not the reason why consciousness withdraws from the world? This retreat of the conscious mind at the critical phase of noonday is the siesta. It is essentially linked with the midday hour, the *hora sexta*, the hour at which the sun reaches its zenith and becomes dangerous to life. We must shun the absolute and disintegrating light, just as we avoid absolute darkness. The desire for sleep is the almost ritual human reaction to the invitation to an absolute creative awareness and vigilance that noon holds out to us. No one can survive a confrontation with the absolute. Everything that is absolute is amorphous and chaotic; man is thus faced with the task of giving shape to the world himself. The siesta is the anti-rite by which man flees this con- frontation and the ensuing crisis.

This retreat before the absolute is typical of human life that flourishes in twilight. We flee from everything that we cannot integrate into our lives, that threatens to disinte- grate them. Wonder and bewilderment are only allowed to attain a certain degree of intensity. When man can no longer integrate them, he no longer absorbs them. The siesta is a specifically human reaction. The birds do not join in and in fact the enjoyment of a siesta is heightened by the sound of the sparrows twittering in the eaves or the hens busily cackling in the yard. Let the animals stand guard over things in the afternoon. They do not know what it is to stand face to face with reality. This is why they can defy the noonday devil and represent man at this critical moment.

Even without the influence of these primitive ideas, the siesta is thought of as a flight. This is obvious from the way in which the phenomenon is treated. On the one hand, we try to view the afternoon nap as a purely physical affair, something that occurs quite automatically at a certain time after the midday meal—and why, for that matter, so much more insistently in summer than in winter—and on the other, since we are evidently hard put to explain so human an activity with physiology, we attempt to excuse it by inventing all sorts of pet names for it and by adapting circumstances so that there can in fact be no question of sleep. The siesta is not sleep; we must find a completely different name for it. We do not retire to bed but merely relax in an easy chair. We do not sleep but doze off, take a nap, snatch forty winks, have a snooze, all of which would be unthinkable at night.

The siesta is a small, passive, apologetic anti-rite, enacted during the passing of the noonday devil in order to dim the glare of that terrible light and to keep the ghosts of that light at bay. Here a panic flight from the pitiless clarity of existence without opacity is stylized into a piece of bourgeois culture. And it would be interesting to examine exactly how large is that piece of human culture which has its origin in a flight from bewilderment.

2. The Panic Moment

Bewilderment is panic. From the etymological point of view the word panic is connected with the name of the Arcadian shepherd god Pan. If we consider their meaning there seems to be quite a gap between, on the one hand, the mythological substratum of this adjective and the noun panic and, on the other hand, the ideas commonly associated with these words and which have to do with a sudden, violent fright. For Pan is after all the god of shepherds and of flocks in the landscape in which idylls are usually situated. He protects the flock and makes it thrive. He takes part in the rural life with its idyllic peace. As a modern psychoanalyst, Paul Diel, has said, Pan is a symbol of the naive enjoyment of nature.

Yet Pan is a divinity or a demon, sometimes a *daemon meridianus*. He is neither man nor poet. His character is completely different. As a godhead indeed, he is an incarnation of that which is totally different, numinous. The idyllic representation of his character and of the Arcadian landscape with its inhabitants does not do sufficient justice to this quality in him. The idyll is an urban *Verharmlosung* of the shepherd's life and background. Its sugary, sentimental quality acts as a euphemism or a reconciliation rite. It wards off the danger and is a way of integrating it into the culture. The landscape is numinous presence. The Arcadian landscape is barren, not idyllic. As a pastoral landscape it is by definition a piece of ground where fertility is more sparse than evident, so that the shepherd and his flock must seek for food. The city dweller, who idyllizes and idealizes from a safe distance, would never be able to stand it.

Only the shepherd ventures into this chaos of aridity and noonday heat. It is the shepherd who here, where life is scarcely livable, meets the godhead and is the first to receive the divine revelations. In the myths it is the shepherd who discovers the abandoned prince and the newly born offspring of the gods. He lives on the barren summits of the landscape, surrounded by wild animals and numinous powers. His existence is no idyll but a risky enterpise lived out far from the community and its culture. The shepherd thus is the closest to divine nature and most suited to understand its voice.

Pan, the shepherd god, is no idyllic little goat to play with. He is a demon of barren nature. And that nature is barren in which man cannot exist, which threatens to rob him of his being, which is landscape to such an extent that it immediately annexes and turns into landscape any immanence that ventures into its territory. Nature is at its most barren in the noonday heat. Pan too is then at his most panic and disseminates panic fright. At the moment the sun reaches its zenith, Pan dominates the landscape. This is the panic moment.

It is from this point of view that the usual meaning of the noun and adjective panic can best be understood. These words are commonly associated with concepts such as ter-

ror or fear or alarm. Yet it might be better to speak of bewilderment. Terror is apprehension in the face of an indefinable threat, fear refers to a concrete danger, fright is
usually associated with the sudden feeling of apprehension.
Bewilderment also has this quality. It too occurs suddenly,
in the indivisible moment of a discovery. It cannot be traced
back to a previous state nor can it be associated with one.
This word is one of the key words in the thought of José
Ortega y Gasset. With him it is the attitude of the human
being seized by desperation in the shipwreck of existence
and forms the mainspring of his mental and cultural activities. It leads to introspection.

The word bewilderment is associated with a wandering
in the wilderness, probably from the old English *wildern*,
meaning savage, at the mercy of wild beasts. It indicates
a sense of being lost, uncertain of the way. A medieval
word for this wandering is gadding, meaning to move about
uncertainly. Farmers still use this word. They say that the
cows in the meadow are gadding when they are plagued by
gadflies. This is thus not wandering in the sense of not
knowing a particular, clearly defined road but rather of
knowing no road at all. Gadding is a senseless and therefore
circular movement, proceeding from a total disorientation.
The cows' gadding is a panic movement under the influence
of Pan, a paralyzing panic. It is a wild and disordered flight,
completely without purpose. In this case too people speak
of a panic flight, but this is really a contradiction. Panic
movement is not spatial but immanent, an inner trembling,
a shudder. The wild running of the cow is a spatial expression of confusion and desperation.

Flight toward something is no longer panic, it is the immediate succession of the panic moment, outlet and product
of a decision. No matter how irrational the circular flight, it
is already a sort of rational outlet for panic and paralysis,
for it is at least movement. Panic is actually the moment
of desperation that precedes flight, the brief bewilderment
that produces action of some sort or another as a way out
of an impossible situation. Flight is not panic, in fact it

signifies the end of the panic moment. Flight is a liberation from panic and bewilderment.

Panic thus is merely a moment, a word with various meanings. Moment, for instance, may be called an opening in the stretch of time, an occasion. It may be a decisive moment, a crisis. It may also be the climax or nadir of an experience that of its nature cannot last long—of ecstacy, for example. In all these cases the moment is more than a short-lived segment of an infinite time. Time is not homogeneous like a mathematical line. The moment is a concentrated experience of time, a point at which many lines meet, an instant of particular importance. That word "instant" may be interpreted as the space of time occupied by the twinkling of an eye, a very brief space of time.

It might also indicate a moment of wonder or bewilderment, in which we blink our eyes to protect them, as it were, from a sudden rush of sensation from outside, a flash of lightning penetrating our existence. This invasion from outside is at once perceived and averted *in ictu trepidantis aspectus*, as Augustine says, "in the flash of a trembling glance." A moment is not an arbitrary segment of time. The Latin *momentum* means both motive power and importance. The moment is a point of time that serves as point of departure, impetus, to an action or experience, a transition. Time is not homogenous; there are points of time of greater or lesser importance or, perhaps, time is usually not there at all. It exists only in the instant, the occasion, the moment.

Time is not a continuous line, but space between points, moments. The moment is the smallest segment of time; all about it is emptiness. This is what Heimito von Doderer says in his *Tangente*: "Das meiste des Menschen ist Absenz. Wie die Materie selten ist im Raum, wie die geistige Materie der Positionsfähigkeit zu den Raritäten gehört, so sind duch, ganz analog, die Punkte höchst selten im Leben eines virtuell positions—fähigen Individuums, welche diese virtuelle Potenz manifest werden lassen." The moment is an explosion of possibilities. It is time insofar as it is historic, time in which something happens, something is discovered or received. Not all time is historical and fruitful but only the moment distinct from every other, the instant in which a movement that was not history comes to rest, takes a different direction, or in which two movements cross each other in free fall so that at their point of contact an island of concrete meanings develops in the midst of empty absurdity.

A moment of importance like this, during which man blinks his eyes in order to shut out the glare of total light, is also the panic moment. It is not the flight but the moment of paralyzing indecision that precedes flight or some other form of evasion. What happens in this moment, what comes to a stop in it, is so total and decisive as to be indescribable. An abyss is revealed on which is founded the totality of life. Proceeding from the movement that immediately succeeds it, we might say that the panic moment is the paradox of halt and movement, just as wonder is the simultaneous presence of reception and assimilation, the tautological awareness and furious denial of an occurrence.

Everything moves and everything stands still at the same time, through the same cause and in the same direction, insofar as it is still meaningful to speak in this connection of identities like "at the same time" and "the same." For that too is possible—halting in a certain direction. Viewed in relation to flight, panic is a halt in the direction of flight and a flight toward halting. In the state of panic, halt and flight lose their meaning and identity. As long as flight is inspired by panic it is not a flight in any particular direction, but a troubled, senseless movement toward nowhere in particular. In a certain sense it is its own goal, to regain tranquillity and to unseat disquiet, as it were, in the same way as the gadding cow runs to be rid of the horsefly that is tormenting her. This flight is only a flight from the crisis of panic and has no particular goal. It may thus occur besides in the form of a rapid circular movement, in the shape of any sort of evasion.

Evasion is a nonlinear flight from crisis or panic. Zeal and seriousness, burdening oneself with all sorts of preoccupations, may be just as much an evasion as flight in the more banal sense of running away. There is even a form of evasion that consists in promoting panic, in fleeing toward danger. But in such cases we seek the crisis after having first reduced it, in a process of *Verharmlosung,* to a sham crisis, which we are easily able to deal with while still experiencing the not undesirable Jenseits of crisis and panic. If one wishes to be harsh or pessimistic it is not difficult to discover abundant forms of evasive behavior. The formula of "crisis and evasion" might be applied to a considerable portion of refined cultural baggage and the majority of all our ritual activities, revealing them as no more than a panic flight from crisis. The panic moment provides the negative inspiration for many of our human acts. Culture is to a large extent a panic flight from the confrontation with the paralyzing aridity of the spirit.

The panic that precedes flight is a paralyzing fit of trembling that seizes man. This trembling contains the paradox of a world that trembles, collapses, disintegrates, and at the same time becomes petrified. Or is it man who becomes petrified? He becomes petrified and trembles at the same time. His blood curdles in his veins. Here tremor and petrification fuse into the feeling called "horror" in Latin. This shuddering is at once trembling and numbness, movement and immobility. The impulse to senseless flight struggles with the impulse to complete abandonment and submission. It is a series of shuddering waves of activity and passivity.

The person in a state of panic is the prisoner of the impossibility of his possibilities, the vibrating center of conflicting impulses and possibilities. He is in entire possession of himself at a time when he should give way, or he loses himself completely at the moment when he should retain his self-possession. Such is his state of distraction at the panic moment. In this moment the rhythm of life comes to a halt. Either evasion or rite must set it in motion again or else the living being, like an insect seized by panic, must sham dead until the danger has passed, keep his eyes tight shut, allow the world to pass away.

When the subjective rhythm of life comes to a halt, the objective cosmic rhythm also ceases. The objective and subjective short-circuit. The panic experience is a confrontation and an identification with a panic, paralyzing, and petrifying world.

For this reason the panic moment is also an experience of the numinous. It is the immanent vibration in the things of nature, either positive or negative according to whether it is synthesis or disintegration or the prelude to the infinity of their possibilities. It is the tremor that provokes life or death, the shudder of animation or destruction. The quivering is a coming to one's senses and a reaching out beyond them, an acceptance of the other and a withdrawal from it, an unveiling, a revelation, and a veiling. The numen is the ambivalence of existence in concrete form. The numinous is thus the mysterious in the frontier region in which it is possible for us to experience it, a restless up-and-down movement between an existence *en-soi* and a being *pour-soi*, between materiality and spirit—and, in the religiosity of the Romans, between dynamism and materialism. The numen is the flapping fringe of what lies hidden and unmoved. The numinous moves yet does not move. It is, if one may attribute to these familiar words a meaning different from the usual, a *movens immobile*.

The numinous inspires horror, that quivering and shuddering of panic. Panic provides a direct experience of the numinous so that the moment of panic may at the same time be religious. In this sense we may attain a meaningful interpretation of the classic statement that fear is the source of religion. For this *timor* is indeed a rationalization and *Verharmlosung* of panic horror in the same way that the figures of the gods are a concrete interpretation of the numinous. This must not be taken to mean that man, in his fear of nature, has created protective divinities and that his fear of these gods has led him to perform various rituals and to offer sacrifice. We mean merely that panic is one of the prime categories of religious experience.

Nor is it any the less religious for comprising a negative

moment. In archaic life the negative is an extremely important aspect of the divine. To regard religious life as positive in all its aspects and to see the gods merely as gods
and guardians of morality is to mistake the existential
character of archaic religion. Nothingness, emptiness, the
absurd can also be religious categories and it is, to say the
least, short-sighted to discount philosophers who take
nothingness as the starting point or center of their thought
as being, for this reason, a-religious and a-theistic. We
should first have to know what religion really is in order to
decide how much religion this atheism contains and, for
that matter, how much atheism and nihilism lurk in a religiosity which might, as an institution, be an organized
and ritualized evasion. Modern man may perhaps be more
archaic than we suspect, and vice versa.

The panic moment is the experience of the numinous
bursting through into human existence, of difference into
sameness, of happening into thought. Panic is a wrenching,
a disorientation of a rhythm of life that runs parallel with a
rhythm outside. This parallel constitutes its mystery, which
is why panic is so often an object of rationalization. This too
is an attempt at evasion. Panic, the sudden eruption of an
all-embracing fear which affects everyone it touches, is
unexplainable and is therefore called baseless since it cannot be readily identified with an adequate cause. It is
moreover an inadequate reaction to any danger no matter
how great or how acute. Panic makes no possible contribution to safety; on the contrary, it increases the danger. For
this reason it might rather be called a contribution to
danger.

Yet all these rational considerations cannot detract from
its contagion. On the contrary, the more irrational a
phenomenon the easier it is to understand. It is all the
more contagious and all the more likely to occur collectively.
This explains why panic is so often a collective phenomenon.
It means that everyone feels the constant menace of the
panic moment when his rhythm of life falters and his world
falls part. Crisis has a greater immanent probability than

evasion, danger is easier to see than safety, chaos is more self-evident than the cosmos. To conclude from this that the negative predominates would only make sense if we could determine exactly what the negative is, to what extent it is negative and, especially, for how long it will continue to be so. For we cannot dismiss as negative anything that acquires a positive significance, no matter how long this may take.

3. *The Provocation of Socrates*

If wonder is the beginning of philosophy, then all we have said about the noonday devil, bewilderment, and panic is also connected with philosophy. Bewilderment is the strongest form of wonder. An introduction to wonder is also an introduction to bewilderment, a plunge into bewilderment. Philosophy not only plunges us into bewilderment but tries to make us acclimatized to it. It stretches the moment of bewilderment to cover a whole life span. Philosophy is a challenge to go to the utmost limits in wonder and bewilderment. If it digests them it takes its time about it.

In describing the panic moment we have used the word "gad." Are we really justified in using such a farm word in an argument with philosophical pretensions? I might defend myself by referring to Heidegger who constantly employs dialect and archaic terms in his dissertations. One of his key words, *Anwesen,* by which he means nothing more or less than the being of beings, is an old word for farm. This usage is in line with a tradition that goes back to the origins of Western philosophy. The Greek *ousia* which, as essence or being, is one of the brightest stars in the philosophical linguistic firmament also means farm-(stead), prosperity, or property. There is an agrarian thread running through the whole of philosophy and not only its cosmological aspects. Agri-culture is the oldest and most basic culture there is. "Being" appears to be property, "ground" is earth, "nature" is vital force, "spirit" is vapor. And, apart from all this, a philosophical term is an ordinary

word before it becomes a term and, as such, is more interesting and closer to wonder than as a meaningful technical term. But this is a subject in itself.

To return to our word "gad." The matter in question
already occurs in Socrates in the plainest possible form.
He regards it as the origin and inspiration of his philosophizing. The only thing is, he adopts the standpoint not of
the cow but of the gadfly. Speaking in his own defense before his judges, he says literally:

> And now Athenians, I am not going to argue for my own
> sake, as you may think, but for yours, that you may not sin
> against the God or lightly reject his boon by condemning me.
> For if you kill me you will not easily find another like me
> who, if I may use such a ludicrous figure of speech, am a
> sort of gadfly, given to the state by the God; and the state
> is like a great and noble steed who is tardy in his motions
> owing to his very size and requires to be stirred into life.
>
> I am that gadfly which God has given the state and all
> day long and in all places am always fastening upon you,
> arousing and persuading and reproaching you. And as you
> will not easily find another like me, I would advise you to
> spare me. I dare say that you may feel irritated at being
> suddenly awakened, when you are caught napping; and
> you may think that if you were to strike me dead as Anytus
> advises, which you easily might, then you would sleep on
> for the remainder of your lives, unless God in his care of
> you gives you another gadfly.

Socrates continues to provoke even before his judges, and
he regards this as his task. In this respect he is particularly
self-assured and convinced of his own merit, whereas in
other cases he is inclined to be skeptical and to emphasize
his ignorance. The God himself has given him the task
of arousing his fellow men and of keeping them awake. He
is acting from sacred conviction when he exposes ignorance
and sows bewilderment with his ironical questions.

Socrates is the one who has left the cave and has seen
real things in daylight and now when he tries to return
to the cave and to speak of the true light, the cave dwellers

refuse to accept this. They grow irritated and put Socrates to death. In a certain sense one cannot blame them, for the first effect of his provocative activity is paralyzing and negative. Socrates is a *daemon meridianus* whose questions cause people to panic. One of his partners in conversation compares him to an electric eel. Everything he touches becomes charged with electricity and a source of danger to anyone who uses it incautiously or with too much self-assurance. He drives people into a corner from which they can see no escape. The wonder he incites narrows into a bewilderment from which every easy outlet is then blocked. The only remaining outlet was forceful action against the obstacle itself, resulting in the death of Socrates. The way in which the bewilderment was presented to the audience rendered any other solution impossible.

As we have already said, the cultivation of wonder is not without its dangers. Thought inspired by wonder and finding no outlet but aphonia turns in on itself. It may for a time assume the form of a sort of mysticism of thought, the certainty cultivated to the extreme that thought moves and possesses power, that the thinker is a man apart from the mass in the cave, to a mental pride that has no other foundation than this mysticism of an empty yet passionate thought. In this form thought can again become detatched from wonder and things, and be preached as pure provocation. There are philosophers among whom this mysticism of thought constitutes the core of their philosophy, whose entire thought consists of an impatient and passionate tilting at infinite possibilities that are never experienced other than as a totality. The certainty that everything is different, a certainty granted by wonder, creates first of all a violent dualism, one pole of which, the fact that things are so, is experienced by everybody while the other, the fact that things are or should be different, defies description.

Socrates wrote no books and resolved no questions; he only incited wonder. The systematic, obstinate nature of his ignorance makes him a great philosopher for he created the space where philosophy, displaced as it is, must make and keep its home. There is no end to the task of provoking and arousing even though one cannot be certain of providing any definite answer to the question of what all this alertness is in aid of or what is the significance of a substantiated disquiet. It is useless to cultivate a desperation that shows no prospect of becoming fruitful, since this paralyzes independence and activity. But the desperation in which the citizens of Athens decided to kill Socrates was already in itself a misunderstanding, since it mistook the maieutic character of his influence and preferred immediate violence to fruitful deferment. Or perhaps there was never any question of a choice, despite the solemn session. There was only convulsive rigidity and anxiety for a constituted identity.

The disquiet sown by Socrates was regarded as an attack upon the totality of life, not as a perspective. It was substantiated by being interpreted as an exhortation to a hasty, total change, a clear-cut break thus, and not as the simultaneous presence of "like" in "different." It was interpreted as a slogan to be put into practice, not as a principle of thought. But it is precisely as a principle of thought that this disquiet extends beyond the deferment of its own identity to a peace of a higher order as depicted by Socrates' disciple Plato in the world of Ideas. This disquiet and that vigilance also contain an element of hope and enthusiasm.

Four

IDENTITY DEFERRED

1. Identity

Wonder establishes with certainty that things are so. This moment is clearly distinguishable. I pause in wonder because a thing is as it is, at this moment, and not different. It is precisely the emerging "thusness" of the thing that provokes wonder. It emerges thus; it already existed in the background. There is a movement that gives rise to wonder. The recognition of things as they are is no more than a moment in this movement. The fact that they are as they are is immediately localized in a framework of different possibilities. I wonder that a thing is so only because in this form it is different from what I expected or because it impinges upon my nonthinking self as a strange phenomenon and compels me to think. The realization that a thing is so is the shock that moves me.

Wonder sets thought in motion. This motion is enacted between the state of thusness and "otherness" of what incites my wonder. In wonder, things are no longer what they were and it can thus be said that they lose their identity. Identity is not an unchangeable datum; it is not unchangeable and it is not a datum; it is changeable and brought about. Only when we decide to think no further do things acquire an apparent identity. Identity is but a moment's pause between movements. It does not exist without the attempt from which it must result. Nothing is identical of itself.

The logical proposition which states that A cannot, at the same time and from the same aspect, be different from A, which is considered one of the basic rules of thought, is in fact the principle of nonthinking, the end of thought. It would only be true if thought were to cease. Only when we sleep are things identical; as soon as the cock crows they explode again. This definition is also disputable from a logical point of view since no less than twice it assumes as fact the identity it sets out to define, that is, in the words "at the same time" and "from the same aspect." The simultaneous factor proceeds from the identity of time and does away with the possibility that time itself may be revealed as the "nonidentity" of things.

The logical standpoint is like a "freezing" of a constituted identity which limits and cripples thought before it can move. This effect may indeed be the aim of the rule. Thought must therefore abandon this standpoint in order to move. But this is quite simply not possible, so that the principle of identity must be provisionally retained as a dialectic partner. For it may well be that the logical inconsistence of the principle, as formulated, is precisely connected with this. As a last foundation it can go no further than itself, is forced thus to accept itself as a datum, and is nothing but an impatient stamping in the crumbling soil of its own nature as abyss.

To practice free fall, however, it is necessary to remove this artificially constructed support and foundation, at least experimentally. Thinking begins thus with denial and contradiction. The leap into space is made from the assumption that the identity is not given, that A is not A. This is an essential fact in which human caprice plays hardly any role. This denial is something that happens to thought, that initiates it and sets it in motion from outside. This big bang is the beginning of everything. The experience of non-identity impels human fate. It is not chosen, it can only be radicalized.

Children of three sometimes define things by saying "not" in front of the words with which adults usually refer to them. Chair is not-chair; car is not-car. Everything is different. Psychologists regard this as the first signs of arbitrary independence, clearing a space for itself in a radical manner. They reassure parents that it is merely a phase and will pass. Yet it is the first attempt on the part of thought to escape from the cave, a flash of human genius which may not be pursued. The attempt fails, and acceptance of this failure is rewarded by the harmonious growth of the child. This harmonious growth means acquiescing to identity and matter-of-factness. Without this, no harmony is possible, still less what the psychologists, the comforters in the cave, and the priests of mediocrity call adulthood. Adulthood is the reward for accepting identity as a practical proposition.

The toddler's attempt is repeated, even more energetically, in puberty. It is accompanied by lyrical experiences of such elementary significance that they can consume an entire human life. Yet this experience must be put behind us if we are to lay hands on the bait of promised adulthood. And so the attempt fails again and this time acceptance is rewarded by adulthood, a good job in the cave, and a life without the torment of metaphysical unease. Should the attempt succeed, the rest of our life is considered a failure and the psychologists say understandingly that we have halted at the state of puberty, as though there were a phase of life that could be discarded like an old coat.

Identity is not a principle from which thought must proceed. Thought, like movement, needs nonidentity as a principle. If things cannot exist without identity then we shall be forced to conclude their nonexistence rather than their identity, for it is better that nothing should exist than that thought should cease. We might also say—in order not to be too radical altogether—that mobility of thought aspires to identity as an infinitely postponed result. There is an infinite distance between the trivial and the divine identity of things, even if this is the same. It is in this distance that thought and wonder live and move. There dwells the entire man. Identity covers "twoness," thus nonidentity, even when it is not merely a comparison between two different things, but a statement about one thing. "Die Identität ist also an ihr selbst absolute Nicht-identität," says Hegel.

In this statement A equals A there is now no question of a comparison. A is not compared with A as two "identical" products of the same machine. Nor is A compared with itself as, for example, the way it was yesterday compared with the way it is now. It is put on a par with itself: it is like itself in itself.

Yet this equation is not the ascertaining of a fact that lies outside thought. If it is a work of thought, then thought assimilates its method in the fact of ascertaining; it introduces its mobility. I do not know whether, thinking apart, A is A in itself. As soon as I concern myself with the identity of A, I involve it in my thought. A statement of thought such as occurs in the equation of A with A cannot be accomplished without thought. Anyone who attempts to attribute to it any validity outside thought desires only to put an end to thought.

It is thus meaningless to establish, in thought, that A equals A. For in thought A is equated with itself in the way in which it might be equated or compared with something different. Not only does this process remain confined to qualities, but it also involves that which is outside, substantially different. Heidegger says; "Mit ihm selbst ist jedes A selber dasselbe." The dative curls around A and incorporates something from outside in the identity of A in order to confirm it "Jedes etwas ist ihm selbst Zurück gegeben."

Dative comes from dare, "to give," and this is what Heidegger means when he says that in identity A is given back to itself. Without this giving, which is an act of thought and arbitrary since it is a gift, A is not identical. Identity is thus indeed a "given fact" but not in such a way that it can be quite simply established. Within the principle the "datum" is an independent decision of thought; outside, it may be, insofar as it is meaningful to think about it, a present, a gift or a grace. For this reason too, one may speak of a divine identity as an infinitely deferred end term of thought, in which arbitrary thinking coincides with the great event of being. To establish and confirm an identity a reflection is necessary from A back to A, which basically alters A, at least to A *minus*, perhaps even to B. It is not identical in itself and by virtue of itself but only via the detour that causes it to change.

This sounds like a parodox: A, by changing, becomes identical with itself, but it is a given fact of wonder which we accept as the motive power of thought. Even things must lose their souls in order to gain them. Identity is not granted with A, but is dialectically founded and confirmed, in which process it immediately abolishes itself. In order to be identical with itself, A needs the other and for this must sacrifice its identity. The eye sees everything but itself, the mirror reflects everything but itself, the word formulates everything but itself, weight weighs everything and measure measures everything but itself, each abandoning its own identity in order to acquire its specific meaning—in the same manner, A is everything but A. The eye must await another in order to see itself, the mirror another mirror, the word another word, and A must await *non-A*.

The objective may be raised that these examples are all very different, that measure is an arbitrary choice with a solid foundation within this arbitrariness, while the eye is not; that measurement, weight, and mirror, in the examples given, are at the same time subject and direct object, while A is subject and nominal part of the predicate. To deal with the second objection first, we have no right immediately to attribute a logical or metaphysical significance to linguistic remarks and to make the fact that the verb "to be" has no direct object the cornerstone of our thought. And, regarding the first objection, arbitrariness too is a "datum"; it too has its point of departure in a blind spot where its identity is transformed into a question and its foundation to an abyss. It is no less mysterious than a "datum" of nature.

What we are given, from the point of thought—and that is the only viewpoint—is not identity but nonidentity. "Aussi l'identité de la chose n'en est-elle pas la structure originelle," says Levinas. Nothing exists without the dialectic of identity and nonidentity. The first premise of wonder is the explosion of identity. If wonder is to be the principle of philosophy it must be radicalized. All "taking for granted" must cease. But this "taking for granted" is based upon the principle of identity which is the cornerstone of logic, the phraseology of "matter-of-factness."

Identity is the first concept that thought relinquishes to wonder. The first objective certainly is that everything is different. The *principium identitatis* is the first act of human arbitrariness; the tautology seems to extend across an infinite postponement. It is the first synthetic judgment a priori. The total loss of self-evidence in the explosion of identity is the consequence of this act, the impingement of the "different" on the "same," of passivity on activity. The like cannot exist without the different, identity without the explosion, nor "matter-of-factness" without wonder.

2. *Being and Thought*

"The identity of the being with itself indicates another 'identity,' the belonging together of being and thought, being and man," writes Pöggler in his book on Heidegger's way of thought. "A being may appear in the identity which it has with itself when it is thought of as being, when thus the identity of thought and being occurs." Being and thought belong together, they respond to each other. Heidegger has dealt in delicate detail with this belonging together of being and thought, which may be stressed in various ways.

Globally speaking it is possible to say that being and thought belong together in such a way that no thought is possible without being. Thought responds to being and is nothing other than that response. Thought is entirely dependent on being; being is independent of thought. Broadly speaking this is the essence of philosophical realism.

Philosophical idealism lays the stress quite differently. The belonging together of being and thought is an identity of both in the sense that thought determines and constitutes being. Being is dependent upon thought. The mystique of thought, to which we have already referred, is given full rein here. Thought reflects on itself and seeks its own identity. Being can then be degraded to a sort of prop which must enable thought to realize this identity and which can then be obliterated. The more being acquires this function, the more arbitrary thought can become and less disturbed by the "different" quality of being. The end of this development is the total victory over wonder and the complete absorption of the "other" or at least of whatever remnants thought has left. Complete idealism becomes inaccessible, an endless solitary mumbling of a self-righteous thought no longer capable of inspiration.

IJsseling has written an instructive book about Heidegger's reflections on the relationship between being and thought, and wonder is its underlying, implicit theme. In it, Heidegger is called "the thinker of thought." This title is not a sort of superlative of the substantive "thinker" but indicates rather that for the "thinker Heidegger" thinking itself was the principal object of his thought. The question that preoccupies him is, What is thought? and this question is indeed the title of one of his most typical and successful works.

One is also to some extent justified in conferring the title "thinker of thought" on Kant, for Heidegger is constantly returning to and reinterpreting his thought. Although pre-Kantian and even pre-Socratic thought is already characterized by self-preoccupation, especially with impassioned thinkers like Heraclitus and Plato (Plato's comparison of the cave is the heart of his philosophy and at the same time a thinking concerned solely with thought), since Kant it has become one of the basic principles of modern philosophy, not only among phenomenologists of divers colors but also among the positivists and analytic thinkers. The *Critique of Pure Reason* deliberately takes thinking itself as the theme of thought and does it in such a way that, since Kant, no one has been able to think about things without first thinking about thought.

Philosophy is the demand for philosophy and there is scarcely a philosopher who has not explicitly stated this demand in the title of one of his works. In this respect Heidegger is by no means isolated. For that matter, thought is probably not isolated in this reflection. The composition of poetry, the poetic manner of thought, also concentrates upon the actual writing of verses, so that we could call many poets "poets of poetry." This need not even be done expressly. Poetry about poetry may ostensibly deal with something quite different from poetry. A love poem by somebody like Vroman may be interpreted as a poem about poetry.

We could continue in this way tracking down reflections on the problems of identity in various forms of art and thought. Reflection has become an attitude of thought which, presumably, must inspire our thoughts about things. It has conjured into life an endless administrative super-structure covering thought and work which sometimes becomes almost autonomous, an object of mockery to creative or restless spirits. And indeed, institutions threaten to lapse into complete nonsense when, for example, a meeting is devoted to drawing up the agenda for that meeting or when a society holds an annual meeting to discuss its liquidation.

It is again the paradox of the blind spot which cannot see itself, but occurring here in a lively working atmosphere and imparting to work the infinity of contemplation. Reflection has almost become the substance of the things themselves, and the quest for method the chief quest of philosophy, if not its entire content. Or rather the quest for method is again part of the quest for a separate identity.

The important thing is not the method of thought but the method of thinking the thought. The art of poetry is no longer the demand for the manner of writing poems, but poetry on poetry itself. Modern painting does not search for new ways of applying paint, but for the identity of its own existence. Philosophy, poetry, and art are absorbed in that question.

In philosophy this attitude of thought can easily lead to a mystique of empty thought to which it is hard to deny the name of philosophy. Yet it is fascinating to see how this fatal circle is punctured by the greatest of modern philosophers. In his book, IJsseling tries to show how the great obscure German succeeds in reaching things through the circle of his reflection. And thought that does not manage to do this remains fettered in mysticism. Plato's thought can be explained as an unsuccessful attempt to attain to things. His thought cannot make sufficient progress to attain its real object. The more authentic this thinking becomes, the more clearly actual things appear to us as unattainable Ideas. If the world is not reached by thought and its method, then method is no longer what it purports to be: a way toward something.

The title of IJsseling's book indicates how Heidegger's thinking about thought remains close to things: thinking and thanking, giving and being, two pairs of concepts between which no contrast is constructed but whose coherence must be demonstrated. The relationship between thought and being constitutes the most important problem in every philosophy. With Heidegger, being is granted in thought, and thought is a grateful commemoration of the fact of being given. There is an interchange between thought and being, not simply identity as with absolute idealists. Nor is it a relationship as between subject and object but a mutual belonging together.

Simple identity or simple duality would paralyze thought as a movement. There is a deferred identity between being and thought in the space of which thought can move. Belonging together is not being together, still less a having to be together imposed from outside, but the tension of a deferred identity. In this deferment the antinomy of thought is resolved. It renders possible a thinking that thinks everything except thought, just as a mirror reflects everything but itself and a word expresses everything but itself, a thought that denies its own identity and on the other hand a thought that thinks only itself, that is pure reflection and identity with itself.

Thought is of necessity present in its own blind spot, its origin and point of departure, and this presence is wonder. It is the experience of a deferred identity in thought itself. Only in the perspective of infinite deferment is the attempt of the blind spot to illumine and to see itself, of the word to express itself, not doomed to total absurdity. Only thus can it be saved from the folly of a stuttering reduplication of its own blind spot in a knowing of knowledge, thinking of thought, etc., and from the paradoxes of a rigid matter-of-factness. For this reflective reduplication is the rope with which the arbitrary nature of thought threatens to hang itself. Ethically too this deferred identity may acquire a great significance and redeem the ethical subject from a crushing immediacy. Thinking hears, observes, and assembles being, and being is in its essence that which provokes thought and discussion. "It [thought] is not grasping but a perpetual receiving. It is not only speaking but first and foremost listening. . . . Being is giving and thought is thanking."

Thought thus constructs no conclusions on the back of being; it is no striding logic, no method aiming to reach a particular goal as quickly as possible. For, of its very nature, thought has already reached its goal, being. As soon as man, the *Da-sein*, becomes receptive to the soundless voice of being and pricks his ears in the openness of being, then he is a real thinker. It is more difficult to think this thought than to say what real thinking is not. Real thinking is not the calculating and overmastering thinking of science, technique, and metaphysics. Thought does not lead to knowledge, says Heidegger in his book on thought, nor does it confer any practical worldly wisdom. It resolves no enigmas and gives no direct force of action. It is a useless, disinterested dalliance with being and thus a becoming implicated in the occurrence that being is.

The fault with which Emmanuel Levinas in his book *Totalité et Infini* reproaches Heidegger, notably that being is featureless—for Levinas the face of being is the face of fellow man in need—and that Heidegger thinks only ontologically and not ethically, is to a great extent disarmed by the interpretative reflections of IJsseling. In his interpretation which is not only clever and skillful but also Heideggerian, Heidegger's thought clearly offers an ethical perspective in the direction of gratitude although perhaps more poetic and individualistic than Levinas would like. On the other hand it is probably tenable longer than the poetically tinged vision of Levinas of the face of the other as the concrete indication of need and ethical invitation. This ethical perspective is implied with the ontology of thinking as thanks. Proceeding from the thought that being is giving, it is possible to elaborate a philosophy of gratitude. On a more day-to-day level Ortega y Gasset too reminds us that man is in everything an heir and that it is this which distinguishes him from the animals. All he has and is has been given to him; man is the creature with a tradition and a history.

We find in Heidegger more penetrating observations concerning tradition to which IJsseling alludes in his interpretation. Words like re-cognize, com-memorate, point the way toward a description of thought as a grateful commemoration of that which has been given. Thought is a wondering dwelling on and paying attention to the occurrence of "giving." If "being" is originally "giving" and "passing on" then thanking too is paying attention to being. If giving is not performed wonderingly and expectantly, receptively and hushed, gathering and attentive, there is no giving at all. Without thought there is no being and man lapses into oblivion. This interpretation is further illustrated by reflections on symbols, primitive thought, myths and rituals. It is important that these things should be associated with philosophical thought. It is precisely in religion that a piece of wonder has been transformed into a culture essential for thought. According to Ricoeur's definition, a symbol is that which provokes thought, it is the place of a long and pensive lingering; the rite is a commemorative repetition of what was done and given in the dawn of time. Thinking about this commemoration is no longer method but a lingering by the things given by tradition.

Heidegger's work, and principally his later work, undoubtedly contains perspectives which might serve as the basis for such an interpretation. *Sein und Zeit* much less so. Here, instead of a grateful acceptance, we hear more of a destruction of history, a negative aspect, an aggressive attitude toward oblivion. Yet even this negative aspect may be regarded as a preparation for a grateful acceptance, or at least a setting in motion of thought and mind. "Der Geist," says Hegel, "ist wesentlich dies, aus seinem Anderssein und aus der Uberwindung dieses Anderseins, durch die negation der negation zu sich selbst zu kommen. Der Geist bringt sich rervor, er macht die Entfremdung seiner selbst durch." Even the establishment of nonidentity has a clearly ethical aspect. It can be based on nothing other than an invitation to a restoration of identity.

The negative is a purification, a methodical clearing of the way to the place where we already are. For the ultimate task of thought is to clarify our place in the deferment. It is not important as a work of art, for its inner consistency, or for the consistency of its method but because it brings the thinker closer to reality. And thought that does not produce this effect is worthless. Emphasis upon this truth determines the value of a pragmatic philosophizing. Thought is a detour to the place we occupy. We are only where we are when we think.

The difficulty of thought arises from the simplicity of this task. The simplest is the most difficult thought to express in words for it runs the most risk of sounding banal. In order to be real thought, simple, original thought must be difficult and follow the detour of negation and destruction. It cannot begin tautologically, but strives towards an infinitely deferred tautological end. Without this difficult struggle against banality and forgetfulness of being we will never reach our goal or conquer what has been given to us. The identity of being and thought is not to be taken as a matter of course; their belonging together spans an infinite distance. Without this distance, being cannot give thought the shock necessary to set it in motion in panic wonder.

3. The Thing

Nonidentity is the moving power of thought. On this point, one might be tempted to say that such an assertion is in conflict with simple experience. Not only can we not perceive nonidentity, but we perceive things in their identity. It is precisely their identity that characterizes things and makes them different from man. In Sartre's terminology man exists as a *pour-soi*, a reflecting consciousness. Things cannot contemplate themselves, have no space in themselves, but exist as a massive *en-soi*; they are crushed on their own identity. To quote Ortega y Gasset they have a clear being and are complete in themselves.

All this assumes that a thing exists of itself, independent of thought. It is the endless and eternal task of thought to think things independent of thought, to propel them as it were out of the circle of thought, and to attain them in their independent existence. The mystery of thought is inspired by this impossible task to leap over its own presence and to attain things where thought no longer exists. It is not for nothing that Plato's Ideas acquire an independent existence. We cannot imagine things except as existing detached from thought and recoiling against thought. In their independent existence things constitute the shock that kindles thought. Their being is by no means purely imaginary for in that case thought would have no cause to wonder about things. The being of things is independent and self-justified and it is just because of this that they are able to startle thought into motion. We can only think of things by thinking of them as existing outside thought, *en-soi* and identical with themselves.

But this independent existence is implied in thought, being its extreme, unattainable limit. Things too have a deferred identity. They are thought and given their independence in that deferment. Whatever is involved in any way at all in the movement of thought, as an object of thought loses its trivial identity. This thing is not the thing; the "other" appears in the "same" as the space in which the thing can be thought. The *en-soi* of things is a product of reflection and thought. The thing is not identical with itself but is identified with itself by man. Identity is an infinitely postponed end term of a reflection. Things do not reflect and are thus not identical with themselves. It is even absurd to speak of a "self" in connection with things. In thought things become implicated in the nonidentity of man which dwells in the deferment. The deferment is the ontological differentiation.

We could put it like this. A spoon is after all a spoon and nothing but a spoon; the different factor is not present in the spoon. This, however, is an optical illusion. I have a Roman bronze spoon which I can distinguish from all other spoons. This distinction is also a differentiation, an extension of its identity. This spoon is not "the" spoon. Yet I know something about "the" spoon; otherwise I would be unable to fix "this" spoon as "a" spoon. It would not possess its identity of "this" spoon without "the" spoon that I know in abstract. The abstract "the" is the nonidentity of the concrete "this." In order to be known, this spoon, which is distinct from every other spoon, has to sacrifice its identity. And yet there is no other spoon like this. How many Roman bronze ladles survive? Their adventures have all been different and all these differences make them uninterchangeable.

This ladle has seen a good deal of use. I can tell this by the way it is worn on the left-hand side, evidently from rubbing against the edge of a pot. I can incidentally conclude from this that even then most people were right-handed and ladled toward their own body. This fact in it-self can incite wonder, since the possibility of left-handed-ness does exist. The spoon is covered with a layer of patina which seems to be the thing with antique bronze. That too is a strange phenomenon, for this alluvial deposit of history really does not belong with the spoon. It would be unhygienic to use it as it is. History and the patina have rendered the ladle unusable.

And what is a utensil that can no longer be used? Does it retain its own identity or has it acquired another? In any case then this new identity is connected with contempla-tion, for the ladle is now solely an object of contemplation. Its patina has turned it into an artistic thing fit to hang on the wall in the sitting room. It is no longer just an ordinary spoon. Considerations quite other than its usefulness as a ladle have now entered the picture, and there is nothing I can do about it, not even if, against all the rules of aesthe-tics, I remove the patina. A Roman ladle is too special for this. It must always remain this ladle, not as it was made but as it has become. Its accidents have overgrown its sub-stance.

But now I clean it after all. I use chemicals to remove the patina and to give the spoon the shape it had when it was still in everyday use. Cleaning makes things respectable, proper. Proper comes from the Latin *proprius*, "own." Clean-ing is a ritual attempt to give things back their own shape, to restore a lost identity. It already presupposes the loss of this identity. The spoon has been involved in a history of people, subject to all sorts of changes. The "other" has constantly intruded into the "same" and set up house there. And the spoon is a technical thing. It represents possibilities, is realized as an arbitrary coming together of possibilities, but is not their definitive realization. Despite this spoon, "the" spoon continues to exist as the denial of this spoon's identity. The "other" is present here.

Heidegger says of the thing that it "things" in the sense of gathers together. It gathers together gods and men,

earth and heaven. It exists in the endless space of a deferred identity. It might have been quite different and it is
essentially involved with other things. The thing is not
simply the thing; it is an object of endless contemplation
since it is itself a concrete infinity. The coincidence of the
establishable "thusness" is no smaller than that of a conceivable "otherness." The discovery of this coincidence or
improbability causes all "taking for granted" to cease and
marks the beginning of wonder.

What actually happens now in wonder at this concrete
thing? In the first place I understand the thing. I see it
assembling before my eyes out of a fan of possibilities, I see
it congeal out of the liquidity of those possibilities and con-
dense to form a separate identity. This is what it means to
understand: to see a concrete thing as the realization of
possibilities. The realization of one possibility never gives
rise to anything concrete, just as an act can never be motivated by one motive. Concrete means formed into a mass,
solidified. The thing is the realization of an indefinite number of possibilities. In wonder I see this realization taking
place. I understand the thing even in its static improbability,
and the greater this improbability the more the wonder
grows. The thing becomes involved in the infinity of a calculation of odds; the dark patch of its concreteness stands
out in a clear void of imagined possibilities.

In the second place, I see the thing shifting into its context where it takes up its place. At that place it is confirmed
in its identity. But that place is its very mobility within the
framework. In that mobility the thing explodes again in
its possibilities. This, too, wonder experiences; it goes up
and down through a melting point; it sees the thing caught
up in a round dance of processes and events in which it
loses its identity time and again.

4. Historism

In this way, with regard to things that have a cultural-
historical context, historism can be understood from the
standpoint of wonder, not as a rigid doctrine but as a way

of continuing wonder, in other words, as true philosophy. We do historism an injustice when we regard it as an objectionable relativism that only attributes to things the meaning they possess at a certain moment in history. Historism is associated with the discovery of history as a dimension of human existence and of evolution as the development of possibilities. Any form of thought that does not take this dimension into account remains divorced from reality. No one can elevate himself above history to a standpoint capable of existing independently of history. Everything exists in time and thus in deferment. Time is deferment itself. Everything is historical. This statement is a direct translation of the thesis that expresses wonder: everything is different. Nothing simply possesses its own identity, sameness and difference are always interacting. History is the dynamics of this nonidentity. Things and people have a history or are themselves history precisely because they are not identical. History is the extension of identity; it is therefore mobility and evolution.

Historism shows us that this assessment is of great philosophical significance since it is derived directly from wonder. Only when historism abandons this wonder and attempts to give things a clearly defined, albeit constantly changing, identity in the different historical periods, does it become doctrinaire and unphilosophical. It is not so in its inspiration nor does it refer to limited historical periods. It is concerned with history as a movement, preferably in the sense of progress. This is how historism appeared to romantic thinkers like Herder, before it became a doctrine with global pretensions.

History is more than a series of events that can be chronicled. It is itself the great event within the extension of identity. It does not reveal being but is actual being in its dynamics. Thought without a historical dimension is a hybrid undertaking with no relation to reality. History as happening is being as the "other" which installs and reveals itself in the "same," and as a way of thinking, history is thought that is suited to this being as happening. There is nothing that is not historical and contingent. It is history that gives things an independence which is constantly jolting thought and setting wonder in motion.

History is the expression of manifold possibilities, not a structure which men imagine of their own accord but a developing reality in which man plays his part. Under his hands the development of possibilities acquires almost automatically the character of an explosion or a free fall whose speed is quadrupled every minute. More happens now in ten years than used to happen in a hundred, and soon more will happen in a year than ever happened. Actuality is becoming increasingly the total history of mankind, experienced in one moment, and it lasts shorter and shorter. People live longer and experience more history in a day than all preceding generations together ever experienced. Identity too explodes in this acceleration of current; it is merely provisional. Everything is different and appears to be different before it can be established that it is so. If we wanted to predict the future from a distance of a couple of hundred years, our prediction would not be valid for much longer than a couple of weeks.

5. *Plato's Theory of Ideas*

We could take the following as an example of purely intellectual wonder. Someone explains to me something of the laws of heredity and describes how an inherited disposition is handed on to posterity. Disposition, however, is a difficult concept. We could say that whatever exists in disposition does not exist, or exists only in a limited manner. The existence of a disposition can only be established when this disposition is realized and is thus no longer a disposition. This too is a point of wonder that is developed in detail in the philosophy of Aristotle. But there is something else. This disposition does in fact exist: inherited disposition is a message, a piece of information transmitted in a particular code. Science appears able to read that code and thus gain power of one of the secrets of nature. But a disturbance can occur in the transmission of this message, called "static." This static influences the message and consequently heredity in a way that has not yet been fathomed.

This is enough for me. I grow completely dizzy and enthusiastic at the prospects that are thus revealed. Something is called into life that has never lived before, a whole province of my indifference is subjected to violent upheaval. Not only does a bright light suddenly appear above a question as vital as heredity now appears to be, but new key words have been flung into my thought: message, information, static. In my enthusiasm I now view not only heredity in the light of information, but everything else.

Everything is information. Everything that exists is knowable insofar as it exists, and communicable insofar as it is knowable. Information is the structure of all that is. If everything is different, the message of how it is different is already contained in things in the form of information which can be deciphered. Nothing arouses such enthusiasm as the knowability of things. In a frenzy of activity all that I know and think is transposed under this new point of view, shuffled about, and adapted to it. Everything changes and adopts a new structure. Everything must be reviewed. But everything is also static, unpredictable, unknowable. Things are curdled lumps of static or, according to the ancient theory of Epicurus and his school, atoms that have diverged from the straight line in free fall and have become impenetrable masses.

The same thing can happen from yet other points of view if I am prepared to leave myself open to jolting. Each day brings with it a new philosophy. Having said this I abandon the concrete key words such as information, history, or evolution, and arrive only at the fervent, albeit indefinable, conviction that "everything is different." This does not mean that there is something "behind" everything, manipulating it, which could be detected with a little effort. It does not even mean that everything is present in every thing. These statements are too dogmatic. It means that thinking about things is an endless movement towards their identity. Nothing is as it appears at first sight. We need a second, a third eye, and so on. The infinite appears within my horizon as that which is completely different, the negation of identity. Things are "other" before becoming what they are. If a thing is what it is this is only via an endless, restless, pendulum movement toward all that it is not. There is an infinite distance between the thing and its identity, the thing itself and the thing as such.

We might say that Plato, in anticipation, calls the end term of this distance Idea. Idea is the thing itself in its identity. Nowhere does Plato express this so clearly as in the parable/story of the cave dwellers which we have already referred to several times and which may be resuméd as follows. Plato imagines people who, from their birth, have been shut up in an underground cave with a wide entrance toward the light. These people are chained by their necks and legs so that they cannot move and can look only at the wall of the cave facing them. Some way behind them a fire burns and between the fire and them is a road along which runs a wall. Along that wall pass people carrying various objects which project above the wall, and also statues of men and animals made of stone and wood and other sorts of material. The fire casts shadows of these images onto the wall in front of the chained men. If now these men could talk and discuss with each other, they would take those shadows for the things themselves, not suspecting the existence of anything else.

But Plato proposes that we should imagine how it would be if one of these prisoners were released from his chains and his ignorance, if he were suddenly compelled to stand up and look at the glare of the fire in the distance. He would not be able to bear its brightness, nor would he be able to distinguish the things of which he had so recently seen the shadows. He would have to grow to accept the fact that those things are more the actual things than were the shadows. And if he were to be dragged out of the cave into the daylight his eyes would be much more painful in the harsh light and only gradually would he learn to distinguish the things of which the objects in the cave were a representation and the shadows a likeness in the second degree. Only then would he rejoice at what he originally experienced as an alienation, and pity the people in the cave. But suppose he should return to the cave. He would not be able to convey to the prisoners there what he had seen. They would not be able to grasp it, would grow angry with him for disturbing them, and would kill him. He for his part would make a ridiculous impression since his eyes would take some time to adapt again to the darkness of the cave.

"This allegory," continues Socrates, for it is he who is speaking, "you may now append to the previous argument; the prison is the world of sight, the light of the fire is the sun, the ascent and vision of the things above you may truly regard as the upward progress of the soul into the intellectual world; that is my poor belief, to which, at your desire, I have given expression. Whether I am right or not, God only knows; but, whether true or false, my opinion is that, in the world of knowledge, the idea of good appears last of all, and is seen only with an effort."

Like every philosophical text this parable is an infinite affair and this infinity is, as it were, quadrupled by the irony with which Socrates expresses even his deepest conviction. It would thus be naive of us to think that the meaning of this passage could be elucidated with a few words. The negative note is clearest. What we see are not the things, for our sight is not acute enough. An infinite progression is possible with the Idea as the end term. Plato's Idea is the extended identity of things. It is not the expression of what is known but of what is not yet known, is reserved for an infinite progression of knowing. "The idea is the guarantee of intelligibility," says De Vries. It is "not the general concept of later logic which, according to many current notions, was raised by Plato to independent existence under the name of 'idea.'"

Idea is the term that expresses the identity of being and thought beyond the extension. It is only the general concept insofar as in it the immediate identity of the concrete is denied and a new identity reserved. This is its own world, the possibility of denying this world. There it is at once the basis of being and knowledge of concrete things. This sounds like technical jargon, yet Plato's theory of Ideas voice an infinite nostalgia for the identity and knowableness of things. He expresses himself ironically because he knows he is talking of something beyond his grasp. The parable contains a clear mystical trait, a fundamental dissatisfaction that things should be so and a stimulus to thought. Plato has absolutely no pretension to a full understanding of Ideas. The Idea of the Good, which is at the basis of being itself, is unattainable; it is the ultimate expression of the unattainable.

Five

WONDER AND ALIENATION

1. Alienation

The parable of the cave has a disturbing effect on our everyday matter-of-fact certainties. It alienates us from them as it alienates the thinker from the nonthinker. Conversation between them is barely possible. Even when they are talking about the same thing they mean something different. Plato says that the man who leaves the cave has to get used to the light outside and, once he is accustomed to it, he is no longer able to find his way and his place in the cave. The philosopher, who has grown accustomed to contemplate ideas, becomes clumsy and ridiculous when confronted with the things of everyday life.

There is a famous anecdote concerning Thales, the earliest Greek philosopher. Entirely absorbed in his contemplation of the night sky, he fell into a pit. A simple, down-to-earth woman helped him out and remarked on the strangeness of his behavior: he was absorbed in what was far away and he was blind to his immediate surroundings. Down the centuries the image of the philosopher and the absent-minded professor has been molded by this sort of anecdote. These anecdotes form the revenge of those who have remained behind in the cave, the way in which they justify staying there. This sort of humor replaces the death penalty and has the same deterrent effect. It is in the same class as the popular opposition of theory to practice in which the latter is held to be more true to life.

Alienation, as represented in these anecdotes, assumes, as it were, the existence of ideas like stars in a distant sky. This image contributes to a wrong interpretation. The ideas are not the cause of the alienation, but a result of it or an outlet from it. They are the things themselves in their identity and conquer the alienation produced by the observation of their nonidentity. The popular concept has the wrong end of the stick. It refuses to acknowledge nonidentity and represents ideas as an aberration of thought. Alienation is the penalty for this aberration. But alienation is an aspect of wonder temporarily located in the space of nonidentity. Ideas are the postulated end terms of a process of identification. They do not exist, but are postulated as a possible means of escape from a wonder which, through the generalization of its motives, results in alienation. The philosopher does not descend from a constituted world of ideas into the banality of each day. It is just that, in his wonder, he is unable for the time being to assign things a place.

In his story of the cave Plato radicalizes wonder and this radicalization is his philosophy. His starting point is observation, as it still is in philosophy. Philosophy is the doctrine of observation. What it is opposed to is stability of observation, an artificial product of life in the cave. Even taken by themselves the revelations concerning the part played by projection in observation are sufficient to jolt this stability. For, as Sierksma pointed out in *De religeuse projectie*, the function of that projection is in fact stabilizing. To see through the projection is to find oneself confronted with the demand for the thing itself, to defer identity. If everything is different then we do not observe things as they are. Observation is the gate through which wonder and alienation gain entry. Our observation is determined by a need for stability. To observe is to select. There are visible things that we do not see, audible things we do not hear, and scents we do not smell. But we have the means of that seeing, hearing, and smelling, and this alienates us from our natural observation. It seems that whole provinces of created things lie beyond our horizon, no matter how close to us they may be.

Plato also makes this point in his parable of the cave and one could vary it as follows. If I, as I now am, were to possess the eyes of a spider, I should view everything quite differently. Not only would I see different things, but I would see the same things differently. I say "different" because, even in my wildest dreams, I cannot imagine what it would be like. I have no idea of it, and idea after all is a word for "that which is different." If then I were to sit here and see in turn with the eyes of a butterfly, a frog, a sparrow, a fish, a hippopotamus, a cow; with rolling faceted eyes, with eyes on stalks, with the dewy eyes of a doe, or even with the eyes of another person, with all sorts of eyes which after all are real eyes and can really see—if, after all this, I were to resume again the very special spectacles of my own eyes on which I rely so blindly, I would feel startled and strange.

There are so many "different" ways of seeing that my own view of things scarcely counts. How many eyes does the world contain? And there are as many worlds as there are pairs of eyes. To realize this is alienation. It shifts me from my own hub and makes me eccentric. This is in fact the philosophic term used to describe the human position with regard to the world; he is outside himself.

Everything is different except that one thing which at this moment happens to appear so. How is reality ever to emerge from this nightmare? As an explosion of "like" into "different." In this way identity becomes an idea in a distant sky, the guarantee of an infinite progression in intelligibility, but also of an endless distance, an endless extension. It is just the loftiness of ideas that condemns thought to an unending alienation. As mobility between the "like" and the "different," in the empty space of nonidentity or of deferred identity, thought is always under the spell of the "other" with its infinite possibilities.

Now it might be objected that there are after all means of registering objectively what the eyes see subjectively. I could, for example, delegate my sight to a camera and then attribute an objective character to the snap. The remarkable thing is that as far as objectivity goes, we are inclined to place more reliance on the machine than on ourselves. When the shop girl rings up something on the cash register, we believe almost blindly that the amount is correct. After all, the machine says so, and it is not in the machine's interest to lie. The machine cannot be wrong. Viewed the other way around, we take what the machine does as the norm for what is feasible; whatever it registers must be all there is to see. What the photo does not show just does not exist in the place photographed or, at least, it is not visible. Anything that is visible is capable of being photographed.

In this way we identify reality with what is mechanically verifiable, thus limiting it to physical reality, but we tend to forget that a camera is a construction of technical man's own hands and can reveal nothing that man himself cannot grasp. If we see a headless man on a photograph we do not assume straightaway that he actually has no head but rather that something is wrong with the photo, and if the adding machine were to announce that two and two are five we would fiddle with it until the result corresponded with our high-handed expectations. Technique thus does not liberate us from our mistakes but rather confirms us in them.

It might also be said that the assumption employed here to illustrate alienation is completely arbitrary. It is merely a capricious quirk of the imagination, not a feasible working hypothesis. Its effect indeed is to paralyze rather than to activate. But wonder too paralyzes. Before it becomes enthusiasm it is panic, bewilderment, and alienation. The Platonic Ideas rescue things and phenomena from the explosion and bring them to safety. "To rescue the phenomena" is a Greek phrase for the philosophical countermovement to alienation, in which things lose their identity. The theory of Ideas is alive to the importance of this movement and thus far (and no farther) has its place in an introduction to wonder. A detailed, philosophical criticism would be something different again. We are concerned only with seeing how this so-called "theory" measures up to wonder, before it becomes a doctrine and a system, not with unearthing "faulty deductions" or whatever.

There is no need to organize a hasty exodus from alienation, nor is this possible. Anyone who has once had experience of "the other" can never quite escape alienation with regard to all that is taken for granted. He will never consent to return to the cave. This fact is associated with the absolute character of wonder as a philosophic principle. Once accepted it can never again be ignored. These are also the sentiments of Kant after he has developed his critical principles: "Wer einmal Kritik gekostet hat, den ekelt auf immer alle dogmatische Gewäsche." And even the arbitrary assumption of an impossible possibility may lead to this alienation. Just as I cannot look with the eyes of a goat, I cannot enter a cave and look at the shadows of statues. Yet this does not detract from the value of this supposition. It serves as a crowbar to dislodge the self-evident.

In the third place, it might be said that the world that is viewed differently through so many eyes is but one world, one and the selfsame world. It is just that this sameness is constantly being viewed differently. But being seen must not be identified with being itself. Here then we are assuming a number of fundamental distinctions, between the substantial and the incidental, between observation and thought, etc., which imply a whole system. But that system was constructed for the very purpose of surmounting alienation and making it easier to digest, to integrate that which is "different" or to oust it. It is not right to use a system to refute alienation which in fact inspired that system. Alienation is not based upon systematically marshaled arguments nor can it be abolished by them. It can only be undone and even changed into enthusiasm by a prospect of identity.

2. *The Inspiration of Dualism*

Perhaps we have not done full justice to Plato's theory of Ideas. I may have committed a philological error in my interpretation of the story of the cave or failed to take sufficient account of other texts in which the Ideas are dealt with more dogmatically or systematically. But I was concerned with the inspiration, not with the system. It is even doubtful whether Plato has a system. In any event the cohesion of his thoughts does not form a closed system and part of that cohesion is so playful that his theories on immortality, anamnesis, and preexistence which are all connected with his teaching on ideas must of necessity be implicated in that playfulness and irony. We can choose between an interpretation which gropes toward a living point and a short, dogmatic resumé which excludes all wonder.

We have already sketched such a resumé in the introduction. It might also run something like this: "To the changeable world Plato contrasts unchangeable Ideas which exist of themselves. They conform to all concepts of species and are above space and time. Ideas are the only true reality. Knowledge of reality is knowledge of the Ideas in the image of which reality is molded." Such a resumé need not be inaccurate in order to be meaningless. Yet it does Plato an injustice in every respect if it says nothing of his inspiration. If it is true that Western philosophy is a series of footnotes to the work of Plato, it would be advisable to talk less dogmatically and self-assuredly about Plato and Platonism.

A sentence such as I have been accustomed to quote deserves a little philosophy to itself. It conjures up an endless wonder and alienation concerning the peculiar development and stagnation of what passes for philosophy. There are forces at work in philosophy as a whole, whose sole aim is to cause philosophy to stagnate. Systems are often called Platonic which have no earthly connection with Plato. Granted, anyone who reads Plato without a feeling for literature and without a sense of humor, who simply takes him at his word as though he were uttering an important statement or compiling a scientific report, will indeed manage to distil a system from his works, but it will be nothing but a parody. The name of Plato is frequently bandied about, but few people have read him.

Nowadays, anyone who has made any progress at all in psychology cannot give a lecture without attacking Plato for his dualism. He is regarded more or less as the direct cause of all twentieth-century ills, just as though nothing had happened in the intervening twenty-four centuries. But his dualism is not of the kind that makes people feel compelled to defend him in the present day. It is not a static and systematic datum but a dialectic principle which serves as springboard for an intellect that, while aggressive and radical, is yet playful and mercilessly dissects the world of phenomena. It is the tension between the cave in which we are incarcerated and the world of which we suspect the existence, between real and unreal.

People think too little before they discuss Platonism. In its coarsened and dogmatized but completely unplatonic form the system is too easily communicable to give rise to profound philosophical reflection. His whole life long Plato tried to prevent this misunderstanding. He would not consent to having his "real" doctrine written down because he knew it would be an impossible task. This is why he entrusted his thoughts only to the flowing streams of playful dialogues. Yet even this could not save them from a coarsening systematization.

This dualism, which is on everyone's lips in connection with his philosophy, was much less doctrinaire and dogmatic with him than one would gather from the manuals. In fact, it becomes true dualism only when it is separated from wonder. But then it is no longer philosophy and has no meaning as dualism. In reality, we are dealing not with two independent and contrasting things but with a tension within identity. Dualism is a condition of wonder. It is the ambiguity of that which is the same yet different in the space of nonidentity, the "between" of a breach. If A is not identical to A, then a dualism already exists between A

and *A*. The inspiration of this dualism is the nonidentity, the loss of self-evidence. There is dualism in the restive, deferred identity of thought and being. Wherever there is nonidentity, thought is inspired to a form of dualism. Anything that can be thought, cannot simply be thought; it inspires thought. There is a gap that must be bridged. That which is, is not identical with being.

This is the ontological distinction, the prime difference and source of the deferment. The other transcends the like just as that which happens rises above that which is, and this transcendence again contains distance and duality, even between things one would like to identify. The method for this identification is not a way but a leap across the abyss of deferment. At an expression of nonidentity, dualism is a necessity and a source of inspiration. Thought is so accustomed to being motivated by nonidentity that a deferred identity is expressed as a duality. Body and soul are sometimes contrasted as two things, each with its own identity.

Yet it may be that we are dealing here with the deferred identity of something whose nonidentity has been so plain from the outset that linguistic usage has chosen a different word for the two sides of the empty space within that nonidentity. Linguistic identity does not necessarily mean factual identity; different names can be given to the deferred identity of the same thing. The relationship of deferred identity can exist between language and reality itself. Language may be the distance of things with regard to itself in thought, a function of the void which gives rise to reflection.

In this way the relationship between matter and spirit, real and unreal, body and soul, reality and idea could be that of nonidentical and identical. To note their duality is not to pin them down but to establish a dynamic principle, a dialectic motive which makes thought possible. Dualism in its origin and inspiration is thus quite different and much more than dualism as a vehemently condemned system. As soon as it becomes a system it has already abandoned its origin and is no longer philosophy. It is for this reason, and not for any pernicious content, that it would merit condemnation. For only then, as slag and cinders, does it become indigestible and capable of leading men's minds astray. When contrasts are integrated into a system, smoothed over, and made easy, thinking ends too soon. It ends in fact where it should begin—with duality.

Thought's task is to keep the heavens open rather than to construct a system, and this task is unending. This is why thought does not finish with the clear flash which denotes the beginning of an ardent but infertile mystique of thought, a purposeless vigilance, or a dead-end alienation, but is rather a task without end. In the system this end is sought prematurely; it is an abbreviated and hasty way of thought, a form of violence. Thought that begins with a spark or a flash progresses slowly. This slowness is the only way of making alienation endurable.

3. The System as Game and as Endeavor

A system can develop from dualism when it falls into the hands of someone who does not take wonder as his starting point, but prefers administrative work in the office of a constituted philosophy. The system is a product of reasoning, and reasoning is thought without wonder. It is calculation, construction, an intellectual do-it-yourself kit. He who reasons moves at least one step away from the reality which fascinated him in the beginning. Or perhaps system only seems to be all this in which case it is a philosophical game, a playful attempt to conquer a paralyzing bewilderment and to stand on equal footing with a world-ground which according to an old view is playing its game with the world. The basis of things is an unfathomable abyss and anyone who wants to get to the bottom of things must take this abyss into account.

Plato gives clear examples of such a playful systemization that desires to reach beyond wonder and construct its own world independently. He has to play along since, as a philosopher, he does not believe in the seriousness of the reasoning that takes no account of things. Thus, from wonder, he deduces Ideas and grants seeming an independent existence, apart from thought.

Once that is done knowledge can be explained as a flaring up in the soul of Ideas already contemplated, as a recollection or anamnesis. In order to elaborate this, yet another theory about the soul is thought up, this time with dualistic inspiration. The soul must be something capable of existing independently of the body. Recollection is then explained by the fact that the soul already existed before its union with the body. In the history of philosophy this anterior existence is called preexistence. Immortality can easily be associated with it and once we have accepted that the soul continues to exist we must accept the hereafter, an expression of the nonidentity of the world, a world capable of existing by itself in which the separate soul can dwell. In this way reasoning leads us to construct a whole house of cards built up of theories.

Plato was in part able to go along with religious concepts which existed in his time and from which philosophy was engaged in emancipating itself. But the whole thing is a game just as the religious fable is a game. In order to compare it with wonder we must contain each reasoning at its first link and bring each following point then separately back to zero to see it develop from there. Wonder does not reason; it is direct contemplation. Philosophy is not a construction. Ideas develop from wonder but their independent existence does not arise from this source. It results from a trend toward the concrete in speech and imagination. We might almost say the system arises from a mythological manner of speaking. Ideas exist insofar as they are valid in thought, but they do not exist independently of it in the sense that they may be found in any place by any means. The independent existence of Ideas is the specific manner in which they are valid. When we lose sight of this distinction in speaking of Ideas, we lapse into mythology.

In Plato the myth, to a large extent, occupies the place of systematic reasoning. It is language, kept to its word elevated to an independent order and alienated from identity with thought. In mythology, identity is attributed to things because language can do as it likes, without criticism. What is said is again said to be so, just as on hearing a good story we gain the illusion, despite ourselves, that what is being told is actually happening and that we are present. But just as the force of telling cannot make a thing so, the possibility of saying something does not mean that what is spoken of necessarily exists. The identity between language and thought, between thought and being, between word and thing is not self-evident but deferred.

In this, Plato is deliberately frivolous and his frivolity shows a hint of skepticism with regard to serious, i.e., operating in series, reasoning. Only the first link of such a series is valid from the viewpoint of wonder and even this validity is not yet a firm basis upon which to erect whole edifices but only the direct contact with living thought. If philosophy is the radicalization of wonder then it cannot depart one step from it, not even when in the process of radicalization that wonder assumes the form of alienation or loathing. Every second step is a step into mythology and thus may only be taken in the somewhat frivolous and skeptical awareness that it possesses no validity. Should the philosopher lose this awareness, then he becomes serious in the unfavorable sense that Sartre gives to the term; he begins to identify his thoughts with words. When the philosopher radicalizes wonder he must consistently refuse to take a step in the direction of self-evidence as offered by the system. He must be continually on his guard against the attractions of mythology or, as Wittgenstein puts it, "Philosophy is a fight against the bewitching of our mind by means of language."

The system may become the material refuge in which the thinker protects himself against the negative effect of alienation and loathing. A system like that of Hegel's does indeed contain something of the maternal and anyone who accepts it feels safe. Even the retention of wonder is taken care of. Hegel's system is one of the most grandiose conceptions of the human mind. It is a space in which the infinite extension of identity itself is integrated. But it is also conquered and rendered innocuous. An infinite extension is brought within the bounds of human possibilities and this, in fact, is impossible. This is the rock upon which every system perishes, the desire to integrate in its own totality the shock which can only come from outside. In this it shows itself to be blind to reality. There is no way in which the shock can be integrated into a system.

Now we must be careful not to turn the tables by insisting that all reasoning and systematization is worthless or that we must opt for alienation. We must not, out of resistance and alienation with regard to the system, make a system of that very alienation. We are talking here not about the totality of life but about the inspiration of philosophical thought. Science, technique, and life are all impossible without some system. They are built upon reasoning and series; they are based upon unambiguous information. But we are dealing here not with a technical or scientific system but with a philosophical system. It is the task of philosophy to remain as close as possible to wonder. This is a very specific and demanding task which is not valid for everyone and at every moment of the day. A wonder that is not experienced in the perspective of this task can lead to meaningless disintegration.

The task of science is completely different. It is essentially an outlet from wonder, not via ideas or reasoning alone but by using the material at hand. Philosophy believes in things; science enters into things and introduces its own provisional order.

4. Word and Term

We have referred in passing to the distinction between word and term. This was in connection with the use of the farmer's word "gad" which means a purposeless running around and which is used to express the immanent movement at the moment of panic. This word was transferred from cows to human thought and from rushing about to a frenzied search for an outlet. There is thus no question of narrowing its meaning. The word has not become a technical term since it has not been inserted into a system. Its meaning was expanded rather than limited; the broader meaning does not exclude the first, original meaning.

This is not so with the Greek *ousia* which means both "possession" and "being." In the latter meaning it has become a philosophical term in which the notion of "possession" no longer plays a role. "Possession" and "being" are two separate things which more or less coincidentally happen to be denoted by the same word. So at least it would appear, for it would not be difficult to trace the transition from, and with it the link between, the first to the second meaning. This might contribute to the concrete nature of the philosophical vocabulary but it would render a disservice to the system. Within the system a word may become divorced from its original meaning and its real force. It is not the least striking peculiarity of a constituted philosophy that it employs common words "differently." And this "difference" has here nothing of the infinity that characterizes it in wonder, but a very specific limitation, a sign function that is used unambiguously as a reference. The different quality of the word becomes the "like" quality of the term.

There is a clear and explicit distinction between a symbol and a sign. This difference can be located in the indicative character of both. The sign refers unambiguously to a reality outside itself. It is not this reality; it is not a reality at all. As a sign it is a fabrication of thought. It replaces a reality that cannot appear in the situation in which the sign operates. It is an abbreviated rendering of a reality. Its meaning is established capriciously and arbitrarily.

The symbol does not refer to an external reality. It is itself the reality to which it refers. The symbol thus is not a fabrication on the part of thought but rather a summons to thought, a reality which sets one thinking. A reality becomes a symbol because it makes us think or, rather, a thing becomes a symbol. That to which it refers as a symbol is the thing itself, but in the perspective of a new identity. Symbolic thought does not make a different thing of the thing that has become a symbol but situates it according to its meaning within the perspective of reality as a whole. As a symbol the thing is more explicitly present as a reality yet remains itself the end term of thought, in its own identity. The symbol refers only insofar as it is not identical as thing (but even then it refers to itself) to the "other" in its own identity. When the thing that is bread becomes a symbol it does not, in its symbolic form, refer to another thing, but merely becomes more explicitly the thing that it is, situated within the perspective of total reality. The symbol thus is used as a reference but in a manner quite different from the sign.

We might now attempt to make this same distinction in the reality of language. The cases are entirely parallel. The word, like the thing, is a symbol. As a symbol the word is identical with the thing and refers to the same reality in which it only acquires its own perspective. In language, the word corresponds to the symbol, and the term, the technical term, to the sign. The word, like the symbol, has many meanings; the term, like the sign, has only one. And, just as, when viewed from the standpoint of wondering thought, the sign is a fallen, emaciated, and alienated symbol, so the term is a fallen word. It is an artificial product, the result of an arbitrary approach to and overpowering of reality. The term is a dead word, worked out and ossified: it retains only one meaning in which it has settled entire and unambiguously. If it is not used in this meaning the word degenerated to term is used inaccurately. Accuracy is a degenerate and emaciated yet usable form of truth. It is truth on the level of calculation and unambiguity. Truth is sought in thought, accuracy in calculating. Accuracy is made by calculation; truth is kept free by thought.

The word "technical" as the usual adjective accompanying "term" indicates this arbitrary character of sign, term, and accuracy. The term owes its singular meaning to the same circumstances that guarantee to accuracy its clarity and comprehensibility, namely to the intervention of man seeking a way out of alienation with regard to the whole of reality. Term, sign, and accuracy are products of a human activity which shaves off one aspect of reality which can then be approached and classified with ease. Admittedly what one is then approaching is not reality, yet the product of man's interference is clear, unambiguous, and easy to grasp. Chemistry approaches salt and replaces it by the term NaCl. But this is not salt; this is a chemical formula. Salt is something quite different. Chemistry does not approach salt itself in its identity; it is a method of disengaging a term from that identity. This term is only meaningful to chemists. The term thus can have only one meaning insofar as the reality to which it refers as a sign has been reduced to a workable unambiguity by human intervention.

This means that terms do not exist naturally. Words do not originate as terms but are made into terms in the course of history to suit the demands of scientific unambiguity. Once a word becomes a term it loses its life in favor of this lack of ambiguity. For life, any form of life, consists of a vibration of multiple meaning in itself, an immanent vibration, a movement between opposite poles and divergent possibilities of meaning. Life is enacted in the space of extended identity. With the word the loss of manifold meaning also accompanies the loss of the prospective identity of word and thing. Word and thing are only identical as symbols. The term is by no means identical with the reality or aspect of reality to which it refers: it functions merely as an arbitrary sign. Every technical term could be replaced by another. Its meaning is based solely on agreement and upon the logic of having a certain system in the methodical exploration of reality. The meaning of the term tends more and more to focus on a certain aspect of reality.

The word, on the other hand, when considered with care, acquires the meaning of an entire world. A term is not considered and cannot be considered, since consideration is only possible when there is more than one meaning in question. A term can be used without thinking, like a number, and this is indeed necessary within the domain of the self-evident, for it must be as reliable as a figure and not need always to be created anew. We can count terms; they have no other syntax than the method of the technique that employs them. But to count words is to rob them of their life. Words have their own syntax, the order of the language in which all words are given their full due. This order is quite different from an arithmetical manipulation. To a certain extent it is identical with the impenetrable order of reality itself. And it is precisely this unmanipulated, total reality to which thought sees itself opposed. In thought thus, the use of terms is quite a different matter from in the sciences. Science is its own foundation and can thus achieve unambiguity. Philosophy always remains ambiguous and dependent.

Six

THE HUMAN MEASURE

1. The Measure of a Problem

There seems to be no measure to philosophy. It refuses to limit itself to the one-sidedness of a scientific approach to certain aspects of reality, but attempts to cope with reality as a whole. It employs measureless words like "being," "all," "the world." It plunges into a wonder, a bewilderment, an alienation from which there is no way out, or else constructs gigantic systems which constantly collapse under the pressure of history and new thought. Yet it is precisely this fact that indicates some measure. The word measure has two meanings: yardstick or criterion and limitation, curtailment, moderation. Has philosophy a measure, a criterion, and does it keep within bounds?

Measure is necessary even to keep one's ground in chaos. Measure always contains a remnant of measurelessness. Measure cannot measure itself and the agreement by which it measures is a constantly repeated opposition to a lack of moderaton. This arbitrary agreement has reduced immeasurability to one thing and that is the measure itself. A choice must be made between the arbitrariness of this agreement and complete immeasurability. Measuring and measure thus always retain the immeasurable as a birth trauma; this immeasurability is always present in measure just as the eye sees only by virtue of its blind spot. The identical other which is used as the measure of measure and the weight of weight is not the same as them. The variation of measure is as endless as the extension of identity.

Every age has not only its own problems but also a certain measure, a degree of intensity which determines the amount of time that thought may devote to these problems. A methodical limitation is imposed upon inquiry. Our age sees its questions curtailed by the scientific ideal. People no longer seek to know the origin of everything, no matter what. Origin is a word that belongs almost to the realm of myths. The demand for origin is too greedy and too indiscreet, and the question of the origin of everything, posed just like that in the isolation of thought, scarcely seems meaningful to us any more. And yet we know more about "origin" than ever before. But this knowledge is always in reply to the classical human questions, even though the physicists' theory about the "big bang" also holds considerable attraction for philosophical speculation.

Aurelius Augustine was one of these classical greedy questioners. In his *Confessions*, prayer and question succeed each other. No limit is placed on either the one or the other. He wants to know everything. Now it so happens, if I may introduce a personal note, that I have had a remarkable and painful experience with this book. I tried reading *Confessions* with a class of grammar school students, thinking they would be easily infected by the enthusiasm with which I had read it twenty years before. Pupils are rather inclined this way, either because they want to please the teacher or because they are easy to influence. This time however I met with no success but rather that benevolent sort of disinterestedness with which every teacher will be familiar. I myself was even affected by it and indeed lost much of my former enthusiasm for *Confessions*. One thing especially became clear to me. Augustine's problems are not ours and, as far as we know it, our measure is different. Augustine's problems seem to us immeasurable, quadrupled almost into myth. He wrestles, for example, with the problem of the origin of evil and then links this immediately with things like free will and divine substance. He moves heaven and earth with his pretentious thought.

Now this is something we can no longer do, no matter how philosophically minded we are. It even seems comical to us. If we read in a book that Augustine wrestles with the problem of evil we may not find it all that comic since on reading the name we immediately situate the problem in its historical perspective, in the fourth century A.D. But Tom, Dick or Harry is not allowed to wrestle with the problem of evil. He only succeeds in making himself ridiculous, for there is nothing to wrestle about. If there are any difficulties they can be discussed at a meeting or investigated in a laboratory. Thought is scientific, and science is collectivized. The form of individual dilettante thought practiced by a man like Augustine has become suspect to our modern eyes. We tend almost to regard this questioning somewhat clinically and reduce it to a mental defect. No matter how fundamental his questions may be, they appear strange and mythological to us.

The steep, vertical, and boundless thought of the ancients which, unlike the ironical questioning of Socrates, seems to aim directly at exalted and eternally valid replies has become strange to us, not only as a system but even in its inspiration. They seem indeed to measure the merit of their thought against the unmeasurable nature of a problem. Their philosophical interest seems only to begin at the limits of the human domain. They think beyond these limits in words or terms which have little meaning within the boundaries and thus have little appeal to us. It is not difficult to declare that the earth is nothing compared with the universe, to allow man to be absorbed in God and time in eternity. But the question is: how are we to measure them all? For us the only measure we can comprehend is determined by earth, time, and man. We have no other measure and, even if we had, how could we use it?

One day, when I was discussing Augustine's reasoning

whereby, assuming that the intransient is better than the transient, he comes to the conclusion that God, who is entirely good, must be completely intransient, someone remarked that in that case a pebble must be better than a roast chicken since it is at least less transient. Although a little logical acuteness might be sufficient to refute this idea, the fact remains that for Augustine intransience as such is held in high esteem. This is a truth that we are no longer capable of measuring and the conclusions based on it could be piled stories high without affecting us in the slightest. Intransience appeals to us only as a vital force manifesting itself at this moment. Even the blooming of a tree, although we know it to be short, appears to us intransient if we take the moment as measure of this truth.

This to my mind explains why we tend to think that youth is always right and to accept its ideas (or what pass as such) as the norm for what is modern and represents the intransient life of this moment. This feeling is widespread nowadays. Never has youth been so pampered and made so much of. It represents a moment of clear blossoming in life, and this moment has acquired an almost absolute validity, thanks in part to the communications media which invest it with such intensity. Youth does not determine what is modern because it represents the future and will presently be in a position to lay down the law. Its authority is not an advance or an anticipation of a future validity; it is only valid at this moment.

Maturity on the other hand is unmasked as the myth of a definitive identity. It is becoming increasingly impossible to employ maturity as a norm for human behavior and, once it has become suspect, this norm can easily be shoved aside and ignored as a form of psychological force. Yet it is replaced by an even more tyrannical youth: in other words, immaturity becomes the norm. We may of course object, and it might do no harm to voice these objections, yet this will not change the historical fact. It is thus better to review the consequences of that fact which are pretty painful for much of what the classical thinkers voiced so laboriously, assembled so heroically and courageously.

Modern life completely passes them by, and any call they might make upon the hasty passer-by is blown away in the wind.

A great deal has happened. History has turned values completely upside down. The transient has become the intransient not because it happens to possess other and better qualities besides its transience, but just because it is transient—the distillation of an intense life. What does not pass is worthless and boring for no other reason than that it does not pass. An eternal, intransient truth is a truth at a level on which we do not recognize truth since we cannot taste it and smell it there. "Modern" for us has become another word for "true," almost synonymous with "good" and "reliable." We assume that whatever is done according to modern methods is done well, and by modern nutrition we are inclined to understand good and satisfactory nutrition. Our historism is total. Today may be different from tomorrow, but we can be sure that tomorrow will be better and more modern. What is happening now is short-lived but moves us intensely and is presented to us most vividly and emphatically.

We have become *konsumfreudige* citizens of a welfare state, and consumption is only another way of expressing what is transient and fleeting. The rhythm of our life is not determined by eternal truths but by the depreciation of so-called long-lasting consumer goods. Already a generation does not last much longer than the time it takes to wear out a car, a couple of years. We live in passing, enclosed in a thin sliver of actuality where the silence of eternity does not penetrate. That eternity is inside, for at that moment everything is there and nothing outside. The moment excludes nothing but includes everything. It is everything moving simultaneously.

2. *Transience as Measure*

In the sight of death our life will concentrate upon its smallest aim and that smallest aim is then its brightest blossoming. The small things of life play a more important role than great undertakings in the melancholy of those destined to die. We might ask: what do we find most difficult to part with, what would we like to take with us, what would we like to do before we go? The answers to these questions reveal the most important thing in life, not the high-flown words, the heavy obligations, and the exalted principles. These are the first to be jettisoned. A tree blossoming in the garden, the quiet of a peaceful evening, the pleasure of unexpected visitors—all can make us melancholy beyond measure when viewed in the perspective of death.

Church Fathers like Augustine seek for the eternal value in everything: what is the importance of this in relation to eternity? But we wonder: what has eternity to do with me? Transience is our element, and it has a narrow base. Seldom in my life have I been more touched by a story than I was by the brief history of an old farmer's wife. She knew that she was going to die and accepted the fact with the resignation that had marked her whole life. The only tie that still bound her to life was the fact that her cow was shortly due to calve. She wanted to live to see it.

This sounds like an excuse for putting off the evil day or like one of the stupid choices sometimes made by panic-stricken people. They risk their lives forcing their way into their burning house and emerge bearing only a doll or a comb. Yet there is no parallel here. The whole substance of life is compressed into what is going to happen to the cow. The most superficial proves to be the most essential. The joke is a touching story about a person whom we ought to call pious in the sense of gratefully involved in happenings and things. It is a piety without metaphysical conjuring tricks, without allure, but perhaps the only piety that still appeals to us since it speaks from our own element, that of irretrievable transience. This is what gives life its attraction. We do not desire eternity. Such a desire might explain our resistance to death yet what we wish for is not eternity all at once, immeasurable, so much as one more moment of satiation. The only form of eternity we understand is the ever-repeated postponement of a definitive and eternal departure. We live in this deferment, in the provisional dimension. Eternity is not the fulfilment of our deepest desires but our nightmare.

Even if we could succeed in stretching out our life so that it never ended, even then our element would not be eternity but transience, the series of moments. We are absorbed in it through the rhythm of our life itself which seesaws between extreme possibilities and moves in the postponement of its identity. We need, as it were, the idea of eternity in order to experience transience as a reality. We stand on the frontier. High-sounding words about heaven and eternity are important in the rhythm of life, but they owe some of their importance to the fact that they can be denied. We brace ourselves against eternity which for us, no less than transience, means death, an evaporation in empty space where we have nothing to cling to.

Ideas, like eternity and intransience, impress us to a large extent because they so clearly relate to a world that is not our own. They bring out the homesickness and alienation which overwhelm us in the midst of life. *Media vita in morte sumus*, "in the midst of life we are in death." This line from a melancholy medieval poem does not mean that death may strike any minute, but that even or just when life appears most pleasant we stand on the threshold of eternity and transience. Life is a dialogue between these two, while death is pure eternity. It is said that in death life pays the price for its improbability. The improbable cannot last long; expressed in terms of time it is transient. Eternity is much more probable, but the price paid for this probability is lack of life.

3. *The Measure of a Certainty*

The early theologians and philosophers posed questions which ranged far beyond the domain of human competence. They also provided answers which, by their very solidity, tend to become suspect to us. They did not shrink from elaborating the most detailed descriptions of things no human eye has seen: the origin of the world, life in heaven, the attributes of divinity. These views have been passed down and become commonplace, not only in myths, which have no axe to grind, but in solid dogmas and unrefuted phrases. Sometimes we no longer know who was responsible for these phrases but we may be sure that somebody thought them up at some time and acted by them. Nowadays we wonder what inspired men to these thoughts which are too large for human measure to be accepted as certainties. It seems to me that these large certainties are the magnified form of certain assumptions which, in the eyes of the ancients, had to be accepted before certainty could be attained on a smaller and more human scale. The greater certainties were voiced, laid down, and perpetuated in phrases, while the smaller certainties never got a chance.

Thinking was an exalted occupation. Only the most rarefied subjects, which had in fact little to do with man, were considered fit subjects for philosophy: heaven, eternity, the origin of everything, nature. An enormous net of a prioris was cast in order to catch small certainties. The net has survived in the form of phraseology, but we can no longer make out just what certitudes it contained. The inaccurate assumption that the sun moved round the earth formed part of the web in which many pleasant and comforting certitudes were caught including man's place at the center of the cosmos and at the top of a hierarchically arranged creation. The greater certitude has gone but the smaller lives on, enshrined now within the assumption that man is the culmination point of evolution. Man seems to need a framework of mythological and phraseological certitudes within which he can come to himself and his smaller certitudes.

In all probability those ancient thinkers too were already concerned with these small certitudes but they continued to be preoccupied with the larger embracing framework of a priori assumptions which had first to be established. Classical man lived entirely within such a framework, a harmony of the spheres which ran completely parallel to his small life, although at a great height, in a closed and reassuring firmament. He lived, as the saying goes, according to nature, rocked in the rhythm of a cosmic ordinance. All he had to do was forget that he himself had designed it or, if he was a thinker, to try to perfect this design ad infinitum. The old sages devoted all their time to this task and succeeded in constructing a dense and impressive phraseology covering not the great things of life so much as what lies beyond. Once this phraseology is undermined and the great certitudes menaced, the smaller are exposed in all their nakedness. Then it is said that critical people deprive others of their certainties.

But what value can be attached to a certainty that we relinquish so easily and almost eagerly? It resembles rather a carefully camouflaged uncertainty or an empty space stuffed up with phrases. No one has the right to certainty; to take away a certainty is not a punishable offense especially when this act can be construed as an attempt to arouse interest in the eventual discovery of certainties of human dimensions. The high-sounding phrases about lofty things may well conceal an enormous lack of interest in these same things. Words of wisdom degenerate into phrases because they become isolated from what people really think and are interested in. We buy off thought with phrases.

Yet we must also take disinterestedness seriously and ask ourselves whether it has not a certain right of existence. The greater that right the less we need regret both lack of interest and the crumbling of certainties which were great, protective, yet difficult to sustain. For now there is room, and perhaps enthusiasm, for the small things and the small certainties which hardly gained a hearing in the world-embracing, heaven-storming thought of the ancients. We no longer have the big net of phrases with which to catch them; we must seize them in our own hands. Only a certainty we ourselves have grasped and feel quivering in the palm of our hand like a young bird cannot be taken from us.

4. Wonder as Measure

That wonder is a certainty must be constantly stressed. It is a certainty about the "thisness" of this thing at this moment even though it may well be different at the same moment. It is a constantly shifting affirmation which can never achieve dogmatism. Wonder is given too little place in philosophy. The classical religio-philosophical books like the *Confessions* of St. Augustine give the impression of philosophizing above people's heads, straight up into the air. And yet they are sprinkled with words like "heart" and "emotion." This reassures us of the writer's direct and personal involvement in the matter, even though it has nothing to do with his own life.

Not only does this philosophizing help to design an enveloping frame to life in which individual life can breathe freely and find a perspective for its inner life but, on closer inspection, it can always be seen to express a great and inspired wonder. The frame itself is as measureless as untrammeled wonder which no question daunts. And when we consider the measureless answer side by side with the question we can detect in the answer itself yet another piece of question and wonder. We must measure the answer against the question and wonder and never be tempted to dismiss the question by the positive nature of the answer. For this is the very essence of dogmatism, the confirmation of answers detached both from questions and from wonder.

In classical philosophy the answer is so immense that it may be said to preserve the question. We must interpret the thinking of the classical writers and view their system as an attempt before they can have any meaning for us. If we adopt them as they are and declare them part of our own thought by a decree of will, we transform them into a dead phraseology. And just because classical thought is really thought and not merely traditional knowledge, it is a process and a movement. This movement never ceases in a definitive answer. Every answer must be caught up again in thought.

Admittedly the classical writers often give us cause to suspect them of exaggerated certitude but this is partly a result of their method. They are less concerned with describing the way they think than the results of their thought while we should tend to do the opposite. In this respect the *Confessions* of St. Augustine is a valuable document for it describes a way, even though this description betrays impatience, an eager reaching out for great and definitive results. But there is plainly movement in this thought, inspired by unrest and wonder, and this to our mind determines its authenticity and humanity. It gives us access to this work.

Wonder, being suspended between question and answer, is the human measure of this thought. Wonder halts the question at a frontier that it will never be able to pass in the form of a definitive answer. It prevents the answer from bogging down in dogmatic certitude and phraseology. In a certain sense wonder restores the answer to the question and keeps open the possibility of a different answer. In this way it keeps thought in motion so that it never comes to an end where it finds what it seeks. It ends only when it ceases, when thought stops. In its most minimal and most essential form, philosophy is nothing but the radical expression of wonder, time and again.

There is an infinitely long road which no one can travel to the end. At the beginning of this road the ancients pondered on the great things of life, the intransient ideas, infinity, the gods. Sometimes they succumbed to the temptation of making very positive pronouncements on these things, but we must accept that these statements too were inspired by wonder and are thus not so positive as they appear to be. Considered from the viewpoint of wonder they are rather attempts to keep the road of thought open for the future and perspectives that fill the thinker with enthusiasm.

Here too, even when it appears to be reversed, the old proposition of the sophists that man is the measure of things, of being and nonbeing, finds its confirmation. For man appears to be the measure in his wonder, in which he opens his mind on the frontier between question and answer or doubt and certainty. Without this measure both question and answer become so immeasurable as to be meaningless. Only on this point, wonder, does the immeasurable acquire a human significance. Without it, it becomes a vacuum. "We ourselves," says Lichtenberg, "are the measure of the wonderful. Were we to seek a general measure, the element of wonder would disappear and all things would be equal."

5. *The Measure of a Truth*

Because they have a different measure from the ancients, modern people are not fond of general truths. To us a general truth is true only insofar as it is general. It is a truth that has had to withdraw from every concrete thing and has no connection with anything. What formerly appeared as an exciting horizon of definitive validity is now usually seen only as volatilization. A truth is general that is not true in any particular case and is so little adapted to our concrete experience that it might just as well be called untrue. The general is too big and wide, and this explains our dislike of big words and phrases. We suspect them of concealing untruth, lack of contact with reality.

On closer inspection a general truth appears to be valid only in a fixed heaven a long way away. To the ancients this heaven existed in a much more literal fashion than it does for us; it was close to them as an established order. To a civilization intent upon order and the past, the general was much more concrete than it is to us. We live in the midst of an explosion of possibilities which the ancients never dreamed of. Whatever is valid for us is so for a much shorter term and with many more restrictions. Everything can change from one day to the next. Truth no longer has a roof over its head.

The ancients considered as true what had always been held to be true. For them the impossible was what had never happened and the unpérmissible what had never been done before. This made a system possible, stern but maternal, a logic in which the exception, the special case, had no conclusive force but on the contrary only served to prove the rule. The validity of the rule was exalted above the exception, lay on a higher plane safe from all vicissitudes. The exceptional was mere chance. It did not affect the rule because it originated from a denial of the concrete more than from contact with it.

The point is almost arithmetical. You can only say that two and one make three if you ignore everything that is concrete. You might say that it is impossible to count things because the particular is given with the multiple. And it is quite impossible to count people. "Three people" tells us nothing about those people; their similarity takes no account of their individuality, that which makes them one and thus countable. Counting is aimed against itself and that which is counted. In concrete terms two plus one could be anything, even three hundred, if we are talking of hundreds or of two gross and one dozen. It is only three when applied to nothing; it is only true when it means nothing in particular.

A general truth applies to nothing and might just as well be left unsaid. It can be denied and confirmed with the same ease and lack of scruple. Nothing is true in general. Anything that is true possesses its own truth. But is not this statement itself a general truth? No, for I am seeking the meaning of this generality by denying it, by confining it to a measure that we can grasp. I have no wish to count up to infinity. Things have to be said that cannot be counted and accounted for exactly. This is one of the limitations of general truth. It is made provisionally to accommodate an experience that would otherwise be lost. Perhaps then it would be just as good simply to recount this experience. But recounting also means to count. Unless the recounting is a general truth or capable at least of going on beyond the singular occurrence it too will be lost.

In general truth, we must always seek a long arm able

to reach beyond an experience without which it is worthless. But there is no such thing as a general experience. Every experience is a confrontation with an unexpected happening. We can try to incorporate it into the categories of our own arbitrary nature but then we must speak in general terms and sacrifice the identity of the concrete. This may degenerate into pure verbalism but this danger is always present where words are used without, as it were, being invented on the spot and tailored to the situation.

The word in itself is no measure of truth, only the word in its association with thought, thought that survives the situation and retains the experience of it. This is why the same demands are made of reading and listening as of speaking and writing. Whatever we read badly we make worse than it is. It may well be, therefore, that more experience is contained in the old books full of general truths than we see in them when we read them badly.

6. *Veracity as a Measure*

If we read a thing properly it can happen that an old phrase suddenly acquires a meaning for us. The same thing can happen when circumstances force us to pay attention to that phrase. A general truth suddenly becomes really true because we are in a situation from which we can appreciate the experience that lies at the basis of it. When someone dies suddenly, we appreciate that all men are mortal. That one fact acquires general significance and the fact that it *is* general consoles us. Yet we have this experience seldom, perhaps only when there is no other outlet. The general provides such an outlet from the oppression of events. That which is very exalted and promising gives us space in which to breathe. Heaven comforts us when earth fails, the other life appeals to us only when this life offers no more possibilities.

We must not be too quick to call this unreal, not even when we have become critical of the general, the unending, and the infinite. Veracity is sincerity in the face of all that

may befall us, unpalatable though it may be. Veracity is
often said to be a characteristic of modern man. If this is
so it may not a priori exclude the possibility that in one
situation we may be extremely irritated by general or lofty
statements that in a different situation would move us and
appear to us as confirmation of a thought impossible to
verify in concrete.

Veracity is our measure of truth but we cannot apply
it independently. Not only what we do is true, but also what
happens to us, whatever moves us in spite of ourselves. Now
it is my belief that modern veracity is more active than passive. We prefer to acknowledge what we have done, what
we have been actively involved in, rather than what moves
us secretly either to joy or sadness and what we are helpless
to deal with, despite our principles. Very few will admit to
feeling jealous, since this would betray a secret impotence,
and yet it is certain that jealousy plays a capital role in
society.

Modern veracity as revealed so openly in "Confessions"
of various descriptions is fairly limited in theme and could,
in this respect, learn a great deal from the *Confessions* of
Augustine. A truthfulness that is never painful for the person thinking of or recounting his experiences cannot be
reliable for long. In this, too, veracity is no easy measure
of the truth. It is the only one we have but to measure with
it requires considerable detachment and self-criticism. If
my veracity cannot be applied to myself then it is rather
a sort of self-justification or self-glorification which tries to
attain its goal via a misleading detour. The sole aim of
veracity must be to elevate the truth to a level where it can
find contact with human experience.

It might be better to say that veracity has no clearly defined or definable goal. It is not employed arbitrarily with
the intention of achieving any purpose no matter how noble,
but is rather a disinterested fidelity to the concrete situation,
painful and ambiguous as it may be. There are many il-
lustrations of this in the *Confessions*. The story about the
theft of the pears, in which the author accuses himself of

all kinds of turpitude in a style that to us seems rather tedious and forced, reveals the young Augustine in all his petty cowardice. It even exposes a painful trait in the bishop writing the story and we may assume that the author was sufficiently versed in rhetorical and stylistic artifices not to be aware of this weakness in the story. His emphasis on this point is no *Fehlleistung* obvious only to us modern, "wide-awake" readers, but a voluntary act of painful veracity.

Augustine uses this small and insignificant offense to illustrate his somewhat gloomy view of human nature, to insure, as it were, that the reader should not be enthralled by the epic character of the act itself and feel some degree of admiration for the writer's courage. Augustine does not ask for admiration. He is not writing the story of his own great deeds but examining what has happened to him in his life. He submits his questions to the highest authority. This gives to his veracity an openness that we do not always find in modern confession literature, from the confessions of Rousseau to those of Van het Reve.

While we speak of veracity as our measure just as lyrically as the ancients vaunted their general truth, we manipulate it no less ambiguously. If we take literature as a source of information concerning the spirit of a particular age, we might well regard confession literature as typical of our time. This is not unconnected with a development evident in various aspects of literature. There is development in the novel as a literary form whereby less and less attention is paid to the literary structure, thinking up a story with various characters and situations and all the ensuing logical and psychological requirements. Together all these things form an artificial superstructure in which the writer conceals himself like a philosopher in his system. This can lead to a distortion of truth. But no matter, in the confession the writer bares himself directly, albeit in a literary form. He does not speak through the mouths of fictitious personages.

A second aspect of this veracity is that the writer frees

himself of a pressure, principally moral. The discovery of veracity as a measure is also a discovery of its lack in our own actions. We readily identify ourselves with the moral ideals held up to us. Veracity does not detract from these ideals but enables us to recognize the gap between our behavior and the norm that we apply to this behavior. This gap gives confession literature room to play. And yet this confession is not the same as a humble acknowledgment of individual shortcomings. It may, in pride and self-acclaim, cross the line to strike at the heart of morality itself, the source of so much lack of verity. Confession literature in the modern sense is concerned chiefly with an experiment with morality.

In classical times it was different. In actual fact we cannot really speak of a confession literature as a clearly defined genre. Augustine's *Confessions* are unique, and modern confessions are not a continuation or repetition of this genre by an analogous phenomenon. The genre is exhausted once it has established itself in one work; it does not exist as a continuity. There is thus no continuity between Augustine's confessions and the confessions of a writer like Rousseau. With Augustine the word "confession" means "to give praise" rather than "to admit guilt" or "enumerate faults." Augustine places himself before the face of the Supreme Being and tries to determine his position in view of his history. He praises God for what has happened to him and situates his life within an infinite plan. His confession is a prayer. As he himself says, he confesses his shameful acts in an act of praise to God. Ultimately he regards his life not as something he has wrought himself but as a gift.

This is the significance of his *Confessions*: the work resembles a psalm more than an autobiography. The central figure is not the author but the Almighty. This sets the book apart so that Augustine cannot be considered the founder of a genre or a precursor of Rousseau. Rousseau did not rediscover a forgotten genre; the genre did not exist, despite Augustine, and Abelard's *Historia Calamitatum*. He did however dredge up a splendid title from the romantic and moralistic misapprehensions of his time and use it to voice quite different intentions. The nature of his *Confessions* is linked with a romantic cult of the inner life—*J'ai dévoilé mon intérieur*—and a less theological, more moralistic view of sin. He himself is so much the focus of his confessions that they must inevitably end in self-defense if they are to retain any focus at all. The praise, one of the oldest and most fruitful of literary expressions, which in Augustine's book is addressed to God, here recoils on the author himself. It is an experiment with the proportions of self-importance, a scanning of individual boundaries.

Confession in the modern sense has a different polarity from that of Augustine. It is not a profession before a higher court of appeal and therefore a prayer, but an investigation into the nature of the individual ego contrasted with what is alien in or to it. The veracity which is the measure of this has become detached from the greater framework in which Augustine situated it. This certainly has not made it any easier and this enhances its fascination as an experiment.

7. *Self as Measure*

There is a philosophical side to this experiment. We might say that taking veracity as a yardstick the individual ego of man is of decisive importance; the self is the measure. In the history of philosophy the ego has come to occupy an ever more important place. Although it certainly cannot be said that in idealism self alone is regarded as the measure of all things, a philosophical development toward idealism is inconceivable without an emphatic awareness of self. The road from pre-Socratic speculation toward the existentialist attitude to life runs by way of the discovery and importance attributed to the ego. Socrates already took a decisive step when he deliberately turned from the contemplation of nature and devoted his attention to human life, especially in its ethical aspects. As modern people we cannot shake off the effects of this development and our appreciation of veracity too must certainly be viewed in this perspective. We soon reject truth isolated from human experience and disclaim all responsibility for it. In the same measure in which philosophy expands or contracts into a philosophy of self seeking its own blind spot, it also becomes emotional, a matter for human experience, and thus a fertile ground for wonder.

We are dealing here with emotions so I shall take an example that illustrates the extent to which irrational emotions rule the mind. There are a considerable number of people who suffer from a fear of height. This is a very elementary and deep-rooted feeling which has little connection with a real danger of falling. A person's fear does not increase in proportion to the danger of falling, or to the height. A person standing on a chair or a balcony feels this fear more acutely than a person in an airplane. In my experience the airplane passenger often feels no fear at all. Now it is said that the fear of height disappears when contact with the ground is lost. This may be true, but it tells us very little about the nature of this fear.

It might be truer to say that fear of height is associated with responsibility for one's own balance. As long as I am in contact with the ground, I have to hold on to myself. My life is in my own hands, and I see an abyss of painful possibilities that are all my own possibilities. I have to find my own footing in that abyss, difficult though it may appear. But when I am floating high in the air, I no longer have that responsibility. Possible happenings are more numerous, the danger is greater but harder to imagine. Floating is such a marvelous feeling because it is a being carried and relieves me from all responsibility. The actual danger of falling seems to be of little or no importance in a fear of height; it is only a point of departure. When I am aloft in an airplane, I shed both responsibility and fear. In such a situation there is no question of my assuming responsibility. Independently of the magnitude of the danger, fear evaporates as soon as I can no longer measure the danger with my yardstick. In a certain sense it is worse, more frightening, to fall from a ladder and split one's skull than to fall out of an airplane, since we can imagine pain but not death. A danger can be too great for fear. In such circumstances we recoil from that fear and sometimes discover that we possess a form of courage which we only identify afterwards as courage since at the actual moment it was merely the absence of fear.

The same might also be said of truth. We measure it with our own yardstick, our self. In this case Augustine and Pascal speak of the heart. Theirs is a philosophy of the heart with man's inward self as measure. Guardini defines the significance of the heart for Augustine: "As organ and domain of man as a whole, the inner disposition which responds to value is called 'heart.' By this we do not mean emotion as contrasted with spirit. The heart itself is a spirit but one capable of estimating values as distinguished from that which follows the norm. Spirit which can be set in motion by worth and toward worth. Spirit as bearer of the eros."

The heart is the center of an inner life in which experiences are absorbed and from which contact with the world is made. Anything that touches the heart is real and true and involves me completely. The heart is self in its openness. A classical theory concerning a parallelism between the human and the cosmic world may influence this concept. The heart hears the harmony of the spheres and makes it human. The message of the gods too is received in the heart. The heart is not an arbitrary inner disposition, tragic and withdrawn upon itself, but on the contrary a point, a minimum of self-righteousness, no more than necessary for an independent existence. Only here is man by himself; this is his ego, the measure of his judgment.

Augustine employs the word heart frequently because he wishes to relate so much to his own existence; he wants to gauge everything by that measure. In this he is more eager than we are because he had greater certainties. His heart is not the isolated and sometimes rebellious inner disposition that the ego is with us, but the concretization of a feeling of happiness in a harmonious order. He can permit himself to make other demands of his veracity, and desire that it should coincide with the truth. His ego sought an outlet toward the absolute in which it was almost absorbed. Or, to return to our fear of height: he flew so high that he no longer felt fear and could relinquish responsibility for his own balance.

8. *The Tyranny of the Mediocre*

The framework in which people lived in the olden days was stretched to a superhuman measure, ours to the measure of self and our fellow men. Just as the framework of the ancients could degenerate into a phraseology of exaltation, so ours runs the danger of degenerating into a tyranny of the mediocre. Like everything that has been said here, this too can be illustrated by Plato's story of the cave. In that country of the blind the one-eyed man is king. Whoever is best at predicting which shadow is coming next is a notable figure in the cave. His measure lies on the same level as that of the other cave dwellers. But anyone who has gone from the cave to the world outside and then returns to describe conditions there is not believed because he is using a different standard of measurement. Not only has he become clumsy in the cave, he has become persona non grata. He sows disquiet with his news of a world that is "completely different." He affects the identity of things.

The word mediocre refers to quality or intensity more than to quantity. It is a measure that is decided not from inside, from the tensions affecting self and things, but from outside. It is the absence of an individual measure even within the limitations that the standard of measurement has suffered. None of the modern yardsticks is of itself easier than the old. Veracity is not easier than truth, transience is not more comprehensible than eternity, wonder is not more obvious than certainty, youth does not yet mean real life, topicality and fashion are no guarantee of value.

Human standards of measurement are not suited to being applied automatically. This is what happens in the mediocre so that the human measure is lost again.

This is why mediocrity is tyrannical. Its tyranny consists in a complete exclusion of all that is "different" and with it wonder, alienation, and surprise. One of the most surprising and disconcerting facts of history is the amount of aggression generated by the appearance of anything "different." It is immediately regarded as a threat, no matter how slight its scope. Bloody wars have been fought over the exact wording of a dogma, and even now the very mention of these subjects can cause fits of apoplexy. If I am not mistaken people have been burned alive or excommunicated for eating with a fork instead of with their fingers. In all ages and particularly in our enlightened age of merciless equalization people have been mocked, scorned, and slaughtered because of a slight difference in physical appearance, a somewhat longer nose than average, or a skin color that stamps them as belonging to a minority. Despite all progress it is difficult to establish a decrease in these excesses, indeed they seem rather to be on the increase. Anyone who condemns the Inquisition and the burning of witches forgets the fairly recent murder of millions of Jews, the agonizing question of racial discrimination, and various forms of intolerance.

Wonder at these phenomena can be radicalized in philosophical terms but the picture we are then left with is not too optimistic. It is clear that man, collectively, cannot live in wonder and cannot bear the tension imposed by what is "different." He wants to equalize arbitrarily and integrate or remove the "other." This is the tyranny of the mediocre and from the examples given it is clear that this phenomenon is much less innocent than it seemed. If we were to pose the enormous question of the origin of evil from a modern and human viewpoint, then wonder at this shocking fact could not be ignored. Force, the active desire to equalize, the resolute refusal to put up with any deferment are the roots of evil. Socrates was not far from the mark when he said that all the misery in the world is caused by a lack of philosophy.

Detached from people and things, mediocrity is imposed as a framework into which everyone and everything must fit. This framework acquires the independent power of a supervisory institution in which each individual contribution of jealousy or hatred, immediately absorbed, is quadrupled and channeled. What the ancients called the envy of the gods, an enormous force which prevented them from overstepping their human bounds in *hubris,* is in our time the tyranny of the mediocre which compels everyone to remain in the cave.

Obligation is in this case a more onerous duty than even the most rigid moralists of the old stamp could have devised. Their obligation still had the appearance of a distant ideal, there was room to breathe. But all this is abolished by the tyranny of the mediocre which demands complete unanimous adherence to the latest fashion and kills off anything that threatens it. It bypasses things. For instance, you have to have read a book because everyone is reading it. It is not the book that matters, nor even the reading. You do not have to read it, you have to have read it. Strictly speaking, actual reading is forbidden; it is the having read that counts. The book and all it contains must already belong to the past if they are to have a topical significance on the level of the mediocre. This means that topical is what has just happened, not what is happening; what is past, not what is present. One must therefore not read the book in the sense that one loses oneself in it, pauses perhaps to ponder on some detail, enjoys the book enormously, and learns something from it. This is forbidden by the obligation to have read. Actual reading can have an alienating effect, so must be relegated to the past.

Topicality is the trace left by past events, by the shadows of things in the cave. What matters here is not the actual things or events but to be able to join in the conversation about what is past. We have to have seen a great deal; here again, you note, *have seen,* not *see.* Looking is not recommended, nor is it desirable. To see things worthy of note is merely to verify their existence and tick them off on a list of things to be seen. We need not enjoy them but they have to be in our archives as proof that we have joined in, as a receipt. The only thing laid down in these regulations, is that, whether reading or traveling, we should not leave the cave. The undertakings dictated are small and artificial crises, of which the favorable outcome is already anticipated and programed. They are therefore completely superfluous. We pass by things past. To have read and seen is not a form of having or possession. It means putting something behind one, to be done with it. We have to have "gained" a diploma.

This by no means assumes that we have to know everything on the program for that particular diploma. Only the naive and the old-fashioned cherish this illusion. We need know nothing about all this. Rather, the possession of the diploma means that we can dispense with whatever learning we possessed. Once we have the diploma and the accompanying prestige, knowledge becomes superfluous and even undesirable. Ritual burnings of books take place to signify that we are more prepared to forget our learning than to retain it. Anyone who does retain it and remains close to things is regarded as a black sheep.

Now it may be said that this forgetting is directly connected with the meaningless character of a great deal of what we learn at school, but this is not true. It is not the school that teaches nonsense but the mediocre which requires that school knowledge should be nonsense. Knowledge is not needed in the cave, but the communal having done something and the jettisoning of knowledge. The people in the cave communally and ceremoniously celebrate their ignorance as a guarantee against alienation. The person who has forgotten most is the most cultivated and thus the leader. We are taxed on what we no longer know, on the distance which separates us from actual things and from the danger that their identity will explode before our wondering eyes.

It may well be that some will consider the foregoing pages exaggerated and merely the outpourings of a teacher's fanaticism. It does not need much acuteness for that. More acuteness is necessary to realize that it is becoming increasingly impossible to discuss the intrinsic merits of anything, aside from its significance as something topical or a subject of conversation and aside from its significance as an emotional expression, for example, fanaticism. It is scarcely possible any longer to admire a painting solely for what it means to us. We are continually tyrannized by measures that have nothing to do with the case, for instance, the financial value of the piece or the reputation of the artist. In an evaluation as prescribed by the mediocre, the qualities of the actual work are the last factors to be taken into account. This is quite clearly a reprehensible reversal of the order of things which leads us farther and farther away from things and prevents us from thinking for ourselves.

This development sometimes makes it appear that there are two possibilities, so far as thought is concerned: either to think very exalted and absolute thoughts or not to think at all but "merely to live." This dilemma is naturally false for it is not permitted to man merely to live. "Like" and "other" are the same for him, and his very life on earth is a form of thought.

Seven

DWELLING IN DEFERMENT

1. Interest

The person who wonders is deeply absorbed in the object of his wonder, whether it be the peculiar nature of things or human behavior, not excluding a constituted philosophy. If philosophy is a radicalization of wonder we do it the greatest conceivable injustice by regarding it as a preoccupation divorced from life for people of a mild, speculative disposition.

Speculation is anything but divorced from life, when it is linked with wonder. It is the highest or at least the most intense form of life. To think is to be involved in life to the very verge of one's identity. It is the boldest venture man can undertake and proof of considerable vitality. Statements like *primum vivere, dein philosophari* and the popular contrasts between theory and practice, between the bookworm and the vital outdoor type, are false through and through. They express the tyranny of the mediocre to which no one who has once tasted the delights of thought will yield.

While it may be true that philosophers in the main are

harmless, it is no less true that people have been killed in the name of a misunderstood philosophical idea which had fallen into the hands of the cave dwellers. This is an aspect of wonder that cannot be ignored and that we must also try to radicalize. The philosophy in whose name people are killed is no longer a philosophy, since it has betrayed the sacred suspension between wonder and skepticism and has attempted artificially to realize the identity of thought and being by hacking off a chunk of being. Philosophy is not and can never be political agitation. In situations where it leads to agitation and to war it is as irretrievably alienated from itself as a dogma which gives rise to slaughter. An equally wrong interpretation is to see philosophy merely as a constant exhortation to moderation and tolerance, even though, viewed in the light of war and persecution, such an exhortation is entirely legitimate and a life devoted to this cause can be most meritorious.

It is not the primary task of philosophy to exhort to anything at all. Even if we define its task, as we so often do, as inciting and provocative, philosophy incites and provokes with no clear aim in mind. Philosophy never leaves the stage of wonder and remains contemplative, even when the object of her wonder is war and murder. Philosophical contemplation is an intense form of presence and interest. This presence is passive; it is prepared to experience and to bear the "thusness" of things until the very end. This form of contemplative tolerance represents an important value and signifies the liberation from a great deal of misery. For misery is a product of frenzied activity.

No matter how mysterious war may be, it is not an impersonal happening, but an activity initiated by responsible people, voluntarily undertaken and prepared for with great care and effort. This is an established fact; it is quite impossible to find a "natural" explanation for war, to prove that it is a necessary and unavoidable phenomenon. Even should wars occur "by accident" or due to a tragic misunderstanding they are, by definition, something that could have been prevented or, better still, understood. War is and always will be a human act, or the result of such an act, which could have been avoided.

Yet even as a result, war is of such substantial significance and such an independent order that it cannot simply be traced back to any cause. This means that it can never be entirely the consequence of anything. Even the fact that it is hard to explain is no excuse, since as a human act it lies within the competence of human responsibility. Here the inducement or *occasio* is more decisive than the *causa* or cause. This view is as old as Thucydides.

Establishing this fact is a philosophical act when it is motivated by an intense wonder. In this, that deed loses its identity and it becomes possible to consider it as an alienation from itself. Alienation is a possibility granted with non-identity. Man can lose himself in the endless postponement of his identity when he finds this postponement impossible to bear. Man during time of war is not man; he is alienated from himself. War and intolerance are ways in which man alienates himself from himself and usurps an identity that he cannot justify since it excludes any possibility of postponement.

In war, philosophy may see the coarsened form of a dialectic within identity, already described by Heraclitus as war, the father of all things. But instead of being for the most part a maturing process, it is an independent grasping at individual identity and a panic, blind resistance to the other which, according to the philosophical viewpoint, belongs within the same identity as forming part of that identity. As a form of contemplation, philosophy endures the endless postponement of identity. The Ideas with which, according to Plato, it is concerned involve it infinitely more intensely with life than the most frenzied activity. Philosophy alone makes this postponement bearable. Without philosophy there is nothing about mediocrity, indifference, and force. The very reality of war justifies endless philosophizing even if this means abstaining from all involvement and confining oneself to abstract contemplation. From its origin it is a striving after wisdom, not in the sense of general knowledge but rather in the sense of keeping within bounds even in activity and independence. Wisdom recognizes man's limitations.

Limitation means that the measure has already been laid down and that no measure can be applied arbitrarily. This does not imply any limitation in the human domain or of technical experiment or any fear of the totality of life, but merely a being open in principle to all that is different, a refusal to attribute a definitive identity to anything at all. Limitation means that the postponement is greater than the power of man, and the general character of wisdom or the character of wisdom attributed to general insights does not exist as an object of speculation and calculation, still less as a yardstick for a tyrannical reduction of everything to the same level, but as a possibility of enduring this postponement. Classical wisdom must therefore be considered concrete rather than desirous of competing with science and technology. Nor is it necessary to regard it as a fearful curbing of the independent rights of technical progress or as an a priori attempt to limit it. These limits cannot be established a priori. The only thing that can be established a priori is that everything is different and that identity is unattainable. Wisdom is a vital art and thus, primarily, the art of preserving life. Yet to live is to dwell in deferment and thus to reject any tendency toward the absolute.

Philosophy is interest. A deeper meaning should be attached to this word than it is usually given. Interest is a debased word that is used for various superficial and commercial forms of concern and longing. But these are endless matters, extending over the long deferment. Interest occupies an intermediary position. It is a form of being intensely present in the deferment. In everyday language "interest" has acquired too materialistic a meaning to be used as the equivalent of philosophical interest. Interest is detachment rather than concern. Concern lies within the domain of having and of arbitrary action. When we say that something concerns us, that "something" is already represented in a complete and definitive identity. It already exists; we can avail of it or claim our share of it.

Interest, on the contrary, means being involved with

things in their incompleteness and nonidentity. It means being present in the middle or, as the Latin word says, between. The preposition *inter* is a comparative form of "in"; it is more inward. Interest as being in the middle of something presupposes a multiplicity. This need not be a multiplicity of objects in the midst of which the interested person is present. It might just as well be a duality. The duality that is revealed "more inwardly" could be identity and its negation. No multiplicity is so fascinating and "interesting" as that which occurs within the firmest unity or, in another word, identity.

Here lie the roots of philosophical problems such as the relationship between unity and multiplicity, the general and the particular. The space for deferment lies within identity. As interest, philosophy is the identity of life and thought. Whatever is true of life is also true of philosophy; what determines life, determines philosophy. We must therefore think of philosophy as we think of life, as a movement within the same nonidentity. It is thus not alien from life but, in its true idea, it is the identity of life itself or the force that mediates in the origin of life. In the intermediate state it is an attempt to make the space, which is deferment, habitable.

2. *Dwelling between Two Paradises*

The identity of thought and life is also expressed by the fact that the more thought we give to habitation the more habitation becomes a problem and the more uninhabitable the world grows. The studies to which this thought gives rise are of a more poetic or technical nature depending on whether the author looks to the past or the future as norm for an ideal or even successful habitation. There are two paradises, one in the past and one in the distant future. If we define paradise as the ideal dwelling place, the spatial expression of a given or acquired identity, we can, from the localization of paradise in past and future, thus beyond the verge of accessibility, draw conclusions concerning the inhospitable nature of the present.

To put it a different way: ideal habitation, being truly established anywhere, is mythical whether one situates it in the distant past or the distant future. In this case the past, as the primeval age, represents the mythology of the gift while the future represents the mythology of technical independence. The person who expects salvation in the form of a technology not yet attained is just as much a dreamer as he who idealizes dwelling in the past. So far as we are concerned, neither is attainable. We dwell with what we have in the endless space of deferment.

If we reserve the expression "mythical dwelling" for a dwelling preoccupied with the past, we can adopt the definition given by Tellegen in his book *Wonen als levensvraag*: "The Mythical 'settlement' is in the sign of a given cosmos within which man seeks his 'place' by establishing contact with the means from which the cosmos was formed."

We might also say: mythical dwelling is settling into the parallelism of cosmic and human life, allowing oneself to be rocked to the rhythm of the great mother and to be nourished from her center. This parallelism is no dialectic. It is a transition in progress from an existing and abiding order, to which one need only adapt oneself in order to dwell and in that dwelling be confirmed in one's own identity. Mythical dwelling is thus more a gift than a task; the condition laid down is clear and the dwelling results in a definitive establishment, definitive so long as the conditions are adhered to, in other words, so long as the dweller is prepared to adapt himself to the existing, all-embracing plan. The ethic of mythical dwelling poses only this condition. A stay in Plato's cave would be an example of such dwelling except that we do not call it mythical since it is presented as a deterrent example of total alienation. The dwellers themselves, however, are secure there and it is precisely this nostalgic longing for security that idealizes mythical dwelling. Heidegger's deliberate sojourn on a farm in the Black Forest (four times in all) might be regarded as an example of mythical, retrovert dwelling. Nobody lives like that and it is unlikely that anyone ever did.

This question is not only concerned with an idealized past or with history but transcends the history of dwelling to arrive at dwelling as unity of existence. The collector is not unified and the person who nestles into the parallelism does not yet dwell there. Granted that dwelling is already a form of collection, it is not yet a facile bundling together of what might form a flawless totality but rather an attempt that assumes a rather optimistic faith in the existence and collectability of that totality. The manner in which this accumulation is carried out bears all too clearly the signs of a human construction. The arrangement of contrasts in the form of a cross, a mandala or any other four-armed figure is one of the most archaic attempts to subdue chaos and to render space habitable, but this gesture of power or even this clear thought cannot produce order.

The dualism of same and different can only be expressed geographically in here and there. But this is to simplify matters. The "different" is present in the "same"; the dialectic is enacted within the identity. A mythical dwelling which aims at excluding the "different" geographically is an illusion, a magical attempt to halt the dialectic or shirk a task. For dwelling is also a technical task, that of integrating what is different into what is like or establishing a communication between the two. The cave dweller is he who transforms the place where he happens to dwell into a definitive residence and the norm for all dwelling places. Thinking construction replaces technical construction.

The cave dweller may be compared with the person who halts on the river bank and, instead of building a bridge, regards the river as the frontier of the attainable "other" which is then situated beyond the far bank. There then develops a dualistic theory, which justifies the separation, instead of a bridge which ends it. Where the willingness to build a bridge is lacking and is replaced by a rapidly evolved dualistic attitude to life, there one could dwell mythically. But this would no longer be a human dwelling since the identity of the "one" and the "other" would be replaced by an irrevocable duality. In the bridge, mythical dwelling is abandoned as a hothouse illusion.

Despite the original appearance to the contrary this mythical dwelling is not a datum or even an attainable condition any more than the world picture of which it forms part. The myth of dwelling remains a myth, something to ponder on, not an actual fact. Nobody dwells mythically. Mythical dwelling is an archaic integration rite, to use a phrase of Eliade's, a ritual attempt to establish a totality in unity more than a social fact. It is even a rite because, and to the extent that, it is not a fact. The rite confirms a fact but in so doing makes no distinction between desired and actual facts. Burial confirms death but tries at the same time to elevate and deny it. The rain rite confirms the expectation of coming rain but indirectly denies the presence of rain.

The ritual confirmation is directed against an actual denial or, to put it the other way around, ritual denial implies an actual confirmation. Dwelling within a mythical framework of life is a rite, not a technically established or establishable possibility. The fact the rite of dwelling indirectly denies is that even mythical man is disintegrated and completely alienated. The mythical image of dwelling is a protest against facts and history, a ritual return to prehistoric times, the age of undivided existence and totality. The mythical parallelism is a preceding phase of a much harsher dialectic, and even that word is still too optimistic and pleasant for the reality of dwelling.

History holds no relics of prehistoric times; the multiplicity is not a survival of the unity; dwelling as a displaced person is no reflection of a snug, settled, mythical state. The gulf mentioned in the rite is every bit as absolute as the ritual attempt to bridge it is infinite. There is no "recollection" of prehistoric times since there is no continuity. The philosophy of this "recollection" which has influenced thought from the time of Plato is mythical in inspiration. The denial is not an historical continuation of man's total togetherness in prehistoric times and in myth. It is the "loss" of an identity of which totality is the mythical expression and also the soothing description.

The myth of prehistoric times sketches the misery of

historic man but also alleviates it by representing his loss as one that can be ritually cured. The myth of the fall contains the myth of the redemption. The myth in which the loss of totality and integration is presented says nothing of the "loss" of identity; it reduces fall and loss to a workable level by presenting as fall and loss something that was never present. This makes the lack more bearable and holds out hope of a cure.

Dwelling, establishing oneself is an effort. Anything that tries to establish itself admits in so doing that it is not fixed. The Latin *habitare* is less an intensive than a conative *habere*. It is not yet possession but a continued attempt at acquisition. The same holds good for the other definitions and etymologies of dwelling; in even the most fundamental definition one must supply the idea of "effort."

"To dwell is to be oneself," says Tellegen. The popular conviction that one dwells or is at home wherever one is or can be "oneself" is quite true. The only thing is that being oneself does not consist of performing certain gestures, like taking off one's jacket, emitting a hearty belch, or stretching out in a chair—in short, in doing what one likes. To be oneself is nothing more or less than to establish one's identity, which is not accomplished by performing a number of relaxing rituals. On the contrary, if to dwell means to be oneself, it is establishing one's identity in the world, settling in, staking one's claim. This establishment does not merely imply a clamping to the earth, putting down roots, seeking a settled place for oneself and one's family but, much more fundamentally, establishing one's own identity in oneself. Identical is what is fixed. I can search for a place only for something that exists. If dwelling means merely to occupy a place then there is no problem. The problem lies not in the place or the framework but in the identity of what is established.

Dwelling presents problems that are not primarily of spatial arrangement, architecture, or social justice. It is not in the first place a technical problem. Admittedly, dwelling has been made the subject of an optimistic sort of reflection by committee-type people, who are entirely in their element in this superstructure of organized reflection, combined action, masterminding, closer collaboration for mutual benefit—call it what you will. For them dwelling is a fine problem, on closer inspection even a vital problem which has to be tackled drastically.

There is a great deal of this optimism in Tellegen's book. It is a "contribution" to this tackling on the part of someone who "practices" philosophy. One of the points of departure is that "man must know what dwelling means before he knows how to dwell." If we substitute another word, for instance, "breathing," for dwelling we shall see how dangerous this statement is. For it is rather the reverse that is true: if man wishes to know how to dwell, then he may not know what dwelling is. As soon as man knows what dwelling is he is displaced or, more briefly still, knowledge makes dwelling impossible. Once he knows, man lives in a diaspora and he is himself that dispersal.

"Knowing how to dwell" thus can have no bearing upon dwelling as a form of human existence. At most it can only refer to the building of houses and cities, a technical matter in which the existential problem scarcely arises. Even if life were directly at stake, the problem posed in this manner would not be a vital problem but simply a question of self-preservation without any philosophical significance. The philosophical problems of dwelling have nothing to do with green belts or smoke-free zones, with architecture or town planning. It is a problem that deals with the identity of man. Nor is the inquiry directed at the nature of man, what is man, but at his identity. Is man something, a something that can cling to itself, its eventual being? The demand for being already presupposes existence and identity. It is, compared with the problem which concerns us here, a curious-minded and superficial question.

Dwelling has not become a vital problem by reason of a change in the social and economic structures to which man, as being, must adapt himself. Dwelling poses no problem for a "being," not even for a being so complicated that it can really have no fixed dwelling place, that it is always filled with nostalgia for the distant horizons. Starting from this assumption Bollnow and Van der Kerken describe the problems of dwelling as a sort of polar tension between here and there, inside and outside, security and openness. But that sort of dwelling problem has been always with us, precisely because it is concerned with a "being." It does not explain the topicality of the dwelling problem unless one falls back again on changes in the social structure. On the contrary, dwelling has become a vital problem because the search for being has vanished into the abyss of the quest for identity. In the history of this problem, which has always been latent in so much metaphysical unrest, a point has been reached where it dares pose itself under the mask of a quest for a dwelling place. The discovery of nonidentity has made dwelling a problem. Man must dwell in the emptiness of his nonidentity.

Tellegen gives us a few pointers in this direction; he speaks of "dwelling in a sundered world." "The new structure implies mobility on the part of the dwelling man"; "We live in a world in which customary dwelling and pioneer dwelling are in conflict with each other." And also: "Dwelling has, historically-relatively speaking, come within the domain of human freedom. Man chooses his dwelling place in a living area which satisfies the conditions for dwelling. He also chooses how he shall dwell." In this context I understand "mobility" not as a pleasant commuting between home, work, and recreation but as a somewhat optimistic, organizational word for nonidentity. Tellegen's clear explanations, elegantly curled into a question mark, leave whole areas untouched. He does not pose the decisive question of identity which is precisely what must be confirmed in dwelling and which is denied in mobility. The problem does arise, however, in his expositions on Heidegger. "Heidegger refers modern man back to an example of dwelling as an all-collecting presence in one place." This is a mythical dwelling which has become impossible for mobile man.

Bollnow, Bachelard, and Van der Kerken also cling in fact to an elegiac nostalgia for mythical dwelling, the warm nest in parallelity. They think that man has fallen from that nest whereas the soothing magic of dwelling and building indicate that he never lived there. There is a limit to the conclusions we can draw from history. History itself has to be reviewed. What happens does not merely happen, does not coagulate into facts which can be noted down. Happening is an effort which never appears nicely rounded off in results. Mythical dwelling is not necessarily being at home. Medieval or rural privacy does not automatically mean security. House and privacy may be facts which can be established in history; being at home and secure defy all observation especially by those who are at home and secure. Observation even puts an end to them.

The history of dwelling is thus not one of the gradual displacement of man, but of the attempt to conceal an actual displacement, which again is a symbol of nonidentity, and to conjure its destructive consequences. Added to this, Van der Kerken seems more concerned with justifying than describing dwelling. In fact, mythical dwelling becomes an allegory of a heavenly dwelling so that finally his arguments become sprinkled with capital letters which tyrannize over the preceding small letters. The deferment is dealt with too rapidly, too arbitrarily, and too easily so that even the gift of a Jenseits acquires a faulty matter-of-factness.

Dwelling has always been an attempt to establish and confirm identity. This attempt assumes and is directed against nonidentity, the source of all mobility. Dwelling is not even a gathering together of fragments of a lost identity from their diaspora at a place where one wishes to establish them, but an attempt to found an identity by means of this establishment. The dwelling place, the house settles the question of identity. I live here, here I am linked to an identity. I can be found at this address, and anyone who finds me here confirms my identity. I cannot do this myself since in order to do so I would have to step outside myself with a power that I would have to derive from myself. I do not owe the seriousness and the identity of my existence to myself, still less a belief in myself. My identity is established in the community, that is, rescued from its mobility. Building is putting up a dam against chaos, living in what has been built is reserving the chaos of one's nonidentity for the establishing of identity. In dwelling, substance is nourished and collected in an attempt to establish identity. Dwelling is not simply being oneself, but a ritual which prepares one for becoming oneself, a preparatory ritual.

The house not only protects its occupant from outside influences, cold, rain, lightning, chaos, but also works in reverse. It prevents a burgeoning "security" from evaporating in the emptiness of an infinite surrounding space, gives the chance of life to a chosen aggregation-situation, and starts a dialectic between inside and out. The walls create an inner core as center of an identity that is to be seized, consolidated and, as the years go by, confirmed. In the inside the outside is collected and transformed, made to nourish a hungry urge for identity, made part and parcel of our being. Van der Kerken speaks in detail about this dialectic—and in a fine Hegelian manner. With him, however, the dialectic seems too much a repetition of the mythical parallelity. He seems almost to be dealing with two quantities which could exist independently of this dialectic, or which even in fact exist and which, in order to nip any hint of boredom in the bud and eventually to enrich their own existence, begin to act in concert.

Yet outside only conjures up inside with the dialectic, and what evokes this dialectic between the nonexistent "things," namely, inside and outside, is precisely the fact of nonidentity, principle of life and mobility. Within and without are not granted apart from the dialectic; they do not exist in a state of immobility. They are not two partners who pause before dancing together, but terms in the tension of a mobility. Dwelling and identity are provisionally established in the dialectic of outside and inside. Without dialectic the attempt to establish an identity cannot be made.

Dwelling as being "somewhere" is a dialectic counter-movement against a given being "nowhere." Somewhere and something are seized in order to allow a firm identity to build up about them. When we say that by dwelling in his house man gathers himself together into an identity, we are employing "self" proleptically and identity as another word for a thickly congealed opacity of different qualities which after a long period of apparent unalienability come to be regarded as our own. In this sense dwelling means growing accustomed, forgetting the feeling of being displaced. The house confirms an illusory effort at identity. Possession is interiorized into identity, the past is thickened into being and substance. The house is the parental house which we remember, or our own house which we have built and furnished, a wall around the emptiness of a depersonalized self. "La manière du moi contre l'autre du monde consiste à séjourner, à s'identifier en y existant chez soi." If dwelling is being oneself, this means "avoir l'identité comme contenu. Le moi, ce n'est pas un être qui reste toujours le même, mais l'être dont l'exister consiste à retrouver son identité à travers tout ce que lui arrive." Staying gives substance to what is, turns having into keeping and being into remaining. But remaining does not confer identity. It is, according to Berger, only a defective form of being identical: a form that being identical adopts in the temporal.

One might also say: remaining is an attempt at being identical, for the temporal in which it moves is a deferment of actual identity. Identity in the temporal is equal to nonidentity, for time is itself the manner in which things cease to be what they are. Even in a more permanent form, dwelling is a dwelling in deferment, an attempt. The *habitare* is a constant attempt to have, to consolidate having to staying and staying into identity. This attempt continues because it fails every time.

The house then is the place where this effort can be interrupted. The house is the place where we sleep. All the problems of dwelling are solved in bed and in sleep.

Bollnow has a few fine observations to make about bed which could easily be supplemented from what we have just said. But it would be wrong to seek to solve a problem by forgetting it. We are concerned here with waking and vigils more than with sleeping. It is just as fruitless to persist in dead-end speculation. Even from the philosophical point of view, dwelling is an ethical task. *Ethos* means "common abode" or "custom." Moralists speak of custom as a second nature, not in the sense of a compulsory routine but rather as a task given to human ingenuity where nature goes by default. Ethics is the task of inhabiting the earth, giving and allowing oneself to be given a provisional identity. No one can, by his own efforts alone, give himself an identity, and nobody dwells alone.

Identity as a datum in itself is absurb. It must be relinquished in order to learn to dwell. "Being oneself" is an illusion when it can only be enacted within four walls. The fruitlessness of the attempt at dwelling, at establishing oneself on earth with one's substance and possessions, leads to the discovery of detachment, what is actually present, for with nonidentity is granted detachment as principle of an ethical manner of existence in the midst of those who share our fate. The dialectic between inside and outside which leads to the development of the house is a dialectic between me and the other who confirms my identity. The other identifies me and makes it possible for me to dwell. My identity is an ethical or even legal fact. Its establishment cannot be transferred to a mythical past nor be expected of some technical perfection in the future. It becomes an ethical fact in the uninhabitable present.

3. *Ethics and Wisdom*

The philosophy of dwelling has apparently created a rift in the manner of thinking that finds its alpha and its omega in wonder. There has been a transition from contemplative, speculative thought to ethical, from being to must. How are we to justify this leap from one way of thinking to another?

In every other kind of philosophizing this question proves an insurmountable difficulty. If one thinks in independent chains and series, and in this way gives his thought the outer appearance of being scientific, he must either give the object of his thought concrete shape experimentally and independently, as science does for its object, in this way constructing the "must" himself, or he must at once abandon his scientific pose and have recourse to a higher court of appeal: God, nature, utility, or the general interest. Anyone, however, who takes wonder as his starting point, has no need to construct an ethic. In wonder, ethics is granted in principle and the wisdom that desires philosophy as the radicalization of wonder is an ethical wisdom. It is not correct to reduce this wisdom completely to a well-considered knowledge of rules and compromise solutions, sanctified by tradition, as can only occur in a culture essentially based on tradition.

Wisdom reaches beyond tradition, relativizes tradition, and gives it without fanaticism a place in the deferment. As an ethical interest thus it has no connection with conservatism but rather tends toward the radical in its acceptance of wonder and all that wonder implies. It is associated with resignation but is not identical with it. It is deferred resignation which means that it carries on a constant dialogue wih its opposites, revolt and denial. Without the idea of negation and revolt, resignation is not wisdom but a sign of slavery, unworthy of free man. One might also put it this way: wisdom only consists of resignation when it is nourished by wonder that people and situations should be "so" and thus occupies exactly the same position as revolt. Wisdom is indeed deferred rebellion, and it is wrong, speaking from a cult of activity, to attribute to it a negative value as simple resignation. Wisdom has always stood at the frontier of independent action, wherever it may have lain.

With the nonidentity of things, space is granted in which ethical dwelling must be accomplished. We must do something with things because they are not there. Within the given deferment must is identical with being. Apart from incidental pronouncements by an irascible and arbitrary authority and from the tyranny of the mediocre, the word expresses not an obligation imposed from outside but an urge for identity. Must is the emphatic form of what is so, the same emphatic form as occurs in wonder. What I discover in wonder is not so, but must be so. The Platonic Ideas "must exist" in a certain manner; Plato cannot think other than so. The must is enacted within the space of a rebellious identity between being and thought. The "must" indicates the tension of the great moment in which the identity of things explodes. It is as far removed from arbitrary orders as having is from lacking. The Latin for must, *debere*, is composed of the prefix *de* and *habere*, "to have." It is translated "to possess in dependence" which amounts to roughly the same thing as "lack" in the etymological sense of "to have and not have alternately." The Greeks have the same word for "lack" and "must." We must have what we lack. In this, too, thinking man is not a measure in the sense that he arbitrarily decides what "must" be done or had, but that this "must" is revealed in lacking and longing just as having makes itself known in desire.

Only an arid intellect without any desire could think of associating "must" with the arbitrary decision of a person or institution or with an ambitious will. A must that does not correspond to reason or desire is an ethical absurdity which cannot be tolerated long. Such a must ultimately leads to a crazy cult of obedience and the glorification of authority which are at the back of various forms of war, force, and persecution. The ethical must is a desirous dwelling within the space provided by deferment. But this desire assumes, as it were, an endless passivity; it is the golden edge of wonder which conquers alienation.

Since the time of the pre-Socratic thinkers desire has been preached as an ethical principle, yet there is scarcely any conceivable principle which has given rise to so much misunderstanding. These misunderstandings are probably connected with the tendency to regard self-determination as absolute. Desire is not a state that I can choose arbitrarily from a number of other states; my attitude to it is passive. For this reason alone it is a reliable yardstick. Desire is a gift of the good, a proof of its arrival and a proof that I am dwelling in the right space, a prospect of an enthusiastic and even disinterested existence. Whoever has found his way in the deferment gains desire as his reward and this desire has an ethical character; in it the good attains its provisional identity.

Like being and thought, being and "must" belong together. Their belonging together is their deferred identity. The ethical "to hear" and "to be fitting" are also associated with this belonging together. The etymology of these words is a source of wonder. Every etymological dictionary contains varied information concerning the derivation of the verb "to hear" which is connected with meanings like "to be on the alert" and "to be on one's guard." Less attention is paid to the connection and even the identity between "to hear" and "to be fitting or proper." Ethics is concerned with what is fitting or proper. In popular Dutch usage *behoren*, "to belong," besides its meaning of "to be fitting and prescribed," also has that of "forming part of a whole." Thought thus fits being and forms part of being. *Horen* means "belonging together" before it means "to obey." Whatever belongs together does so on the basis of identity. The belonging together bridges the deferment of identity. Ethical obligation is not a compulsory order imposed from ouside, but an invitation that emanates from things.

Authority is the guarantee that deferment can be borne. It is at best a temporary stopgap in cases where insight and reason might fall short. No authority is so definitive that it can have subjects and create stringent obligations. Duty cares for things in their nonidentity; it is the human attempt to restore things to their identity. This is a detached desire on the part of contemplative and interested man rather than an act of obedience to stern governors. It is impressive yet astonishing to see how, in this respect too, man can alienate himself from himself and degenerate into a feudal slave kissing the heel of his master as he grinds him into the dust. History provides a record of this alienation in its infinite variations, in all of which man attains a remarkable provisional identity.

The slave can be a slave to his marrow so that he is no longer playing the role of slave but is, in the measure of his own possibilities, entirely identified with this state. He can no longer free himself from this alienation of his own accord. His wisdom becomes a resignation in which rebellion no longer has any part. The governor too can become completely the governor as we see him in old portraits. He does not disassociate himself from his strange identity but is cruel, self-assured, crafty, and religious. The historical moment has become absolute in an impenetrable density. The governor cannot act in any other way than as a governor; he cannot imagine any other world than the world as he makes it, any other laws but those laid down by his self-righteousness and a god who is on his side. His wisdom can only exist by virtue of the unchangeable situation and the absurd resignation of those under him. As soon as something happens, as soon as history takes a step forward, the slave's resignation explodes into rebellion which turns on the governor and destroys him. His identity is suppressed force: it is the same energy. The servant and the governor have penetrated so deep into the cave of their a-temporal identification that it seems as if force alone can liberate them from it. Even then they will regard this liberation not as a liberation but rather as an attack upon their identity.

Here the tension between wonder and the status quo can reach a point at which the philosopher tends to become a tyrant who is not solely concerned with inciting wonder but wishes to intervene in history with the light of his insight. The philosopher is constantly exposed to the temptations of force and tyranny, precisely in the measure in which he desires to attribute general validity to his interpretation of existence. There is the famous observation by Marx from his thesis on Feuerbach: "Die Philosophen haben die Welt nur verschieden interpretiert; es kommt darauf an, sie zu verändern." In the sense that he creates a place for the "other" and for the "same" the philosopher has already changed the world and this is the most basic and, measured in practical terms, the most practical change. Anyone who opposes force by force can only, assuming that his force wins, give things another identity, just as arbitrary and short-sighted, which in turn leads to more force.

The philosopher, however, does not have recourse to force, not even on contemplating the most readily accepted and cherished slavery, wretchedness, and alienation. The only means he employs or desires to employ, even when he acts with deliberate ethical intent, is that which is his sole possession: the shock of wonder which cleaves open even the identity of fossilized regents. To be willing and to have the courage to do this is his obligation and desire. Death was the price Socrates had to pay for his continual provocation of authority and the people in the cave, and his death was a very deliberate choice.

We might speak in this connection of heroism but this might do less than justice to Socrates' ethos. The word heroism has been spoiled for us for it has become the honorary title of a form of alienation in which a man is prepared to lay down his life on the orders of governors, in which he puts his blind self-confidence into practice to the paradoxical extent that he gives his life in order to achieve something in that life. In this sense Socrates' death was not heroic; he was neither headstrong nor a slave. His daemon was no governor. Rather was it a desire to which he gave full rein, even unto death, since it was of the very essence of his life. The sacrifice of a cock at his life's end signified a victory of life and light over darkness.

The only force the philosopher knows is the shock of wonder. This shock can be extraordinarily violent and it is one of the tasks of philosophy to oppose this violence to force. It is not philosophy's task to lay down rules that must be obeyed literally and at the double. Ethical precepts have their meaning in the endless deferment. They are not a codex for deeds to be performed and projects to be carried out but pointers toward a perspective or ideal. For this reason alone they cannot permit themselves to be relative but absolute and categorical, as were the Ideas of Plato.

Ethics is enduring the deferment; it is patience. Authority without patience degenerates. Patience and wisdom in an ethical context imply that any deviating behavior can be regarded as a "suffering" at deferment, a short circuit with a too emphatically proclaimed norm. But those who dwell in deferment and can do nothing to alter their situation can hardly do anything but suffer. Plato indeed has his philosopher return to the cave. Philosophy ends with the observation with which it begins. The return to the cave means too that it must proceed to the order of the day. If philosophy does not become alert to everyday reality, it is ethically and philosophically valueless. This is the only goal to which it can lead via an infinitely long detour. It does not leave the philosopher free to walk around like an astonished idiot nor does it elevate him above his fellow men. His dwelling place is the cave. Ethics determines the nature of that dwelling and puts an end to endless thought.

4. Need and Deferment

One of the paradoxical things about being human is that in human life, unlike mathematics, we cannot calculate and measure with the factors of greatness and smallness. We must manipulate them in a very different manner. In a certain sense we might say that, on the human level, smallness and greatness, weakness and strength are identical. The weak is not per se less valuable than the strong; it may even prove more valuable not only despite the fact that it is weak but because of it. The weak may be stronger by its very weakness, the small greater by its smallness. This is only possible on the plane of the human ethos.

In the same way the negative can also have a positive significance, like the crisis that threatens existence itself. The terms negative and positive, small and great, weak and strong cannot be considered valid indications of ethical value. The negative is not of itself less valuable than the positive; the weak may be more valuable than the strong. These terms have no decisive significance but only the qualifications good and bad. This means that in order to judge in a human fashion we must avoid giving a mathematical significance to these terms. It also means that a negative qualification may not be regarded as definitive. When one does not view the negative in its association with the positive, one is using the concept wrongly and will not arrive at an ethical standard. One achieves this standard by first looking for this connection and thus deferring judgment on the value of what appears to be negative. This deferment, this detour, is human.

Like human weakness, need too appears to be something negative; it is nothing but a lack, a certain form of human weakness and imperfection. Man is needy insofar as he is not self-sufficient. Need must not be seen as something provisional which disappears once it has been satisfied. It is essentially peculiar to man. Without need he cannot exist. This also means that no human need can ever perfectly be satisfied. Perfect satisfaction of human need would rob man of his human character. Man discovers himself, his human situation, in his needs and in the longing to satisfy them.

We might also say thus that a man's need is identical with his strength. Need is one of the driving forces of human activity; it is the force that carries man forward. Without needs there would be no undertakings. If man were not conscious of his needs he would not be conscious either of himself or of his human condition. His very lack supplies him with his ethical, cultural, and economic norms. This also entails certain consequences in the satisfaction of human needs. On the human level this satisfaction is indirect. It is deferred and, during the period of deferment, is raised to an ethical and cultural level.

Hunger is a need. A direct satisfaction of hunger is to eat whatever falls to hand, but this is an animal satisfaction. A hungry man does not begin to eat at once but defers his satisfaction. He prepares for this satisfaction by preparing a meal. The preparation of food is typically human. The deferment of the satisfaction of hunger has led to the development of the culinary arts. An immediate satisfaction could never bring this need to a human level. Man, as it were, wishes first to experience hunger in its independence and cultivate it into a pro-visional identity in order to make it an object of his contemplation before he does anything about it. The human element makes its appearance between the need and the deferred satisfaction of that need. The deferment of the need makes the human culture and economy, in which it is not only accepted as a fact but cultivated and embellished.

It is interesting to read what Augustine has to say on this subject. After talking about the Prodigal Son who returns and is therefore loved more by his father than is the son who had stayed at home, and about related biblical motifs such as the lost sheep and the lost drachma, he continues:

> What then is wrought in the soul when one is more delighted to find or to regain the thing which it loved, than if the thing had never been lost? . . . The general triumpheth when he is a conqueror, yet he had not overcome unless first he had fought; and how much the more danger there was in the battle, so much the more joy is there in the triumph. The tempest at sea doth toss the passengers, it threateneth shipwreck and all do wax pale with apprehension of death at hand. But what? The sky groweth clear, the sea is stilled and their joy is great exceedingly because their fear was no less. . . .
>
> Yea, the pleasures of life do men acquire by means of the pain that preceded them; and not only by that pain which cometh upon us unawares, but sometimes by that which we do seek after and procure. There is no delight in eating and drinking, unless the trouble of hunger and thirst do precede. And such as are hard drinkers do willingly eat salt meats that they may put their mouths into a kind of heat, in the quenching of which they find delight. It is the custom too that the spouse already affianced may not instantly be put into the power of her husband, lest he should esteem her the less, seeing that he hath less sighed and longed for her.

Various phenomena in human life may be characterized as a deferment of satisfaction, as a detour toward it. Apart from hunger and the art of cooking we can view other needs and their satisfaction in the light of this deferment. Sexual life is common to both man and animal. What we call eroticism, however, is typically human, the more so the more culturally and ethically differentiated man is. Culture is the ritardando in the satisfaction of needs. This eroticism which is so characteristically human must be viewed as a product of a deferment of sexual satisfaction. During the period of this deferment, between need and satisfaction, is born the typically human and independent quality of sexuality, the attention for the person of the partner, the charming manners, the erotic literature, the love poetry, the tenderness, everything that is regarded as more elevated. We may view this detour as a transparent pretext, but in this case we are taking animal sexuality as the model for the human and denying the typically human character of this detour. Viewed on the human level eroticism is something quite different from a crafty, hypocritical detour toward intercourse. It arises from an autonomous significance attributed to contemplative dallying with the beloved, born of and discovered in the deferment of direct satisfaction. It becomes an independent order.

Deferment thus transforms the need into something human. Deferring the satisfaction of his needs makes a being a human being who dwells in deferment where, by his own independent will, he embarks upon a dialogue with the occurrence. Things acquire their meaning in the culture through the narrow funnel of a crisis. Man may be defined as the being who makes of his needs an object of contemplation in deferring their satisfaction and, in this contemplation, elevates himself to quite a different level from that on which the needs arose. In this contemplation the human level is discovered as an irreducible value.

It is wrong therefore to take animal behavior as a model for human acts and to regard deviations from animal behavior among man as unhealthy. No slogan such as "back to nature" will ever succeed in alienating man from his proper level. Deferment only becomes unhealthy when it becomes tyrannical and practiced unwillingly and out of fear. In such cases, however, the unhealthiness lies not in the deferment but in man's attitude toward it, thus in his attitude toward himself. The man who makes an independent order of the deferment of his needs does not accept himself, does not recognize the true nature of his needs, and seems to want to eradicate them. Such behavior might be viewed as a forcible degeneration of asceticism. Asceticism forms part of human life. It too is linked with the deferment of satisfaction and the cult of identity. It is, as it were, the very art of deferment, intended not to heighten the pleasure of satisfaction to the maximum, but to attain the proper human level. Human life is inconceivable without asceticism for then the satisfaction of needs would cease to be human, and degenerate into tyranny.

Eight

WONDER AND GROUND

1. The Cogito of the Rose

In a profound and witty book, full of paradoxes, Chesterton remarks: "Staring at the sky or the grass or the truths of mathematics or even a new-laid egg, man has a vague feeling like the shadow of that saying of the great Christian philosopher St. Thomas Aquinas, 'Every existence, as such, is good.'"

The first of all philosophical questions arising from the sense of wonder at the existence of things, the question of why there is something and not rather nothing, can be experienced and posed in different ways. Joy in existence is certainly the most positive manner in which man can experience this wonder. This joy is, as it were, the feeling of triumph at the capital fact that that which exists is, that it is not nothing and, viewed from the point of nothingness, seems to have been snatched from nothing. Contrasted with this nothingness, held over the abyss of nothingness, existence appears as something complete and absolute. Whatever else it may be and mean, everything that exists, as such, is good.

Our joy at this fact means that this statement is more than a conclusion arrived at by persistent and logically correct reasoning on the part of a joyless intellect. The goodness of existence is a direct and emotional experience rejecting any motivation. It is even difficult to formulate this experience other than in commonplace terms, since it is a primitive human experience. It is the basis of happiness and joie de vivre. To try to render this basis even more basic is to take the risk of falling into an abyss. This abyss is admittedly present in the experience of existence as a good, but it is present there as something that has been overcome, to which it is impossible to return. This return would be a voluntary destruction of existence, a morbid undertaking.

What then is this existence that, simply to experience, gives a vague but unassailable feeling of happiness to the person undergoing the experience? Whatever it is, it is something absolute which we cannot escape, in the face of which all individual intentions are powerless. We might, however, define a certain aspect of this absoluteness as the bloom.

Blooming must be regarded as the way in which existence reveals its absolute character. Since this experience lies in the border region of mysticism and since the mystic is always the most ready to speak out in these matters. I quote here two lines from Angelus Silesius on the blooming of a rose. He says:

> Die Ros' ist ohn' Warum, sie
> blühet weil sie blühet.
> Sie achtet nicht ihrer selbst,
> fragt nicht ob man sie sieht.

In one of his finest works, *Der Satz vom Grund*, Heidegger has devoted to these lines a number of splendid pages, in which he describes the mystical paradox, the apparent contradiction between the *ohn' Warum* and the *weil* and the nature of the ground referred to here. There is yet another possible method of approach, departing from the phenomenon of blooming. The rose has no why, because it blooms; its blooming is its basis and its why, the sole measure of its existence. The etymology of the verb "to bloom" contains notions such as "to swell" and "to unfold." The growth referred to here is one from inside out, aimed at proportions which appear to be determined by an inner law. The opposite of blooming is a purely quantitative increase or mechanical completion. It is remarkable to note how often Homer uses the word bloom. It is his way of praising and emphasizing the fullness of existence in things not made by human hands. What is made by human hands he always calls well made; what grows is called blooming. Blooming here is the welfare of an established existence. Blooming raises existence to a higher order which the poet proposes as norm.

To bloom is to achieve identity. This is the basis of the sublimating significance of the flower in symbolic thought. The flower is the product of bloom, the symbol of a way of existence, devoid of all dialectic, which experiences a breath-taking moment of fullness above the abyss of nothingness. What the lotus is in Oriental symbolism in the mystery of becoming, a focus of developing powers, the rose is in the West in a mysticism of being, a climax of mysterious having-become-thus. The flower, experienced at this moment, before the thought of transience can turn joy into melancholy—for this thought is secondary, it is an afterthought—is symbolic of the autarchy of satisfied existence. This autarchy now implies that every quest for a basis be rejected. The possibility of this quest is swallowed up in the all-predominating phenomenon of blooming. In and beside blooming there is no room for the crafty sadness of questioning and *grübeln*.

The only possible motivation for blooming is tautology. Tautology expresses identity beyond deferment. It is the lyrical primitive form of philosophical expression and its last word. Philosophy moves between an empty and a full tautology. The rose blooms because it blooms or because and while it blooms. Nothing exists outside this blooming which, as such, is not incorporated in a coherent and calculable causal series. The mystical joy evoked by this tautology is the joy of experiencing absolute identity. In the tautological motivation the fact is referred back to itself in a repeated confirmation that it exists.

The absolute cannot be motivated. Everything that might serve to motivate it is already bound up in the absoluteness of existence. Existence is irreducible. When a philosopher like Sartre emphasizes this fact and concludes from it that existence is meaningless, and not only meaningless but negatively so, this presupposes an attitude of mind that cannot be swayed by reasonable arguments deriving from the joy of existence, and that is itself just as unreasonable and irreducible as joy. Joy rejects such an attitude as categorically as it does the omnipotence of nothingness.

One might go so far as to speak of a double meaninglessness, a negative meaninglessness of the void and a positive one of fullness and blooming, but no reasonable argument can be found to justify choosing either one or the other. For his very attitude renders the void of the mystic in a paradoxical manner a thing of fullness and blossoming. And this indecisiveness which is peculiar to all that lacks meaning contains a comic as well as a tragic element. It is indeed rather laughable to see existentialist authors preoccupied accepting tragic absurdity with a heroic smile on their lips. This is the heroism of the spoiled child who is once deprived of sweets and is then brave enough not to cry. Senselessness, void, lack of certainty, disinterestedness are quite simply the stuff of life. Anyone who wants to protest against this might just as well rebel against the tiresome business of endlessly breathing or against the fact that he only has ten fingers.

The rose knows no reflection and no *cogito*. It blooms because it blooms and is itself no object in its blooming. In blooming there is no gulf between being and consciousness, taking part and refraining. There is no between stage. "Zur Weise, nach der die Rose ist, bedarf es nicht eigens eines Achtens auf sich selbst und d. h. auf all das, was zu ihr gehört, indem es sie bestimmt, d. h. begründet. Sie blühet, weil sie blühet. Zwichen ihr Blühen und die Gründe des Blühens schiebt sich nicht ein Achten auf die Gründe, kraft dessen erst die Gründe jeweils als Gründe sein Könnten." In the existence of that which blooms, no energy is withdrawn from the blooming in order to produce in any way at all an awareness or a recollection of that blooming. The rose knows nothing, pays no attention to itself, and does not ask if anyone sees it.

The child in the flower of his childhood knows nothing, retains nothing. It is identical with itself and founds no reservoir of recollections with energy withdrawn or withheld from the experience of the situation. It is not for nothing that to remember is called "to retain"; it is a withdrawal from the moment of what is due to the moment. Memory is a product of nonidentity and deferment. Blooming is the moment of fullness identical with itself which knows nothing of any history. It has its ground and goal in itself. The endless procession of causality and finality comes to a halt. There is a confrontation between existence *en-soi* and existence *pour-soi;* they seem to coincide.

When we consider the flower, we can take the ground that is forgotten in its blooming very literally; it is the earth. It is not by chance that the word ground has this double meaning. In actual fact there is no question of two meanings. The ground of existence is the earth, bearer of life and embracing all reality. The blooming rose has no why; it blooms because it blooms, and its blooming causes all why to be forgotten. The why of the rose, that which links it with the ground, is the root. Root is cause. The rose, in rejecting any ground of its blooming, makes us forget its roots. This is an essential element in the sublimating symbolism of the flower. It denies its roots and the fact of being rooted. It ignores the earth and the dung in which it is rooted.

There is no continuity between earth and bloom; on the contrary, there is absolute discontinuity. In the fact of blooming, this discontinuity is emphasized and elaborated into a dialectic opposition comparable to that between existence and nothingness. This image is so persistent that it has acquired an almost scientific clarity. Gaston Bachelard says of it: "When one realizes that the dialectic of rotting and growth has been the central thesis of botany for centuries, one understands that the antithesis between flower and dung is just as inspiring in the realm of imagination as in the realm of ideas. This indeed proves that we are dealing here with primitive ideas."

Like causality and finality, activity and passivity coincide in blooming. There is no underlying suggestion of perishing in blooming. It is—and it is in an absolute manner; the verb "to be" has no passive form. Here something is achieved that cannot be explained by a cause and that does not aim at a goal. There is absolute discontinuity with regard to what might be considered in the biological order as work-cause or as aim-cause. Taken as an object of contemplation the rose is not a biological fact. It is the miracle which bursts through every existing and conceivable framework and fits into no series. One can only approach it in wonder; any other attitude would be banal.

Blooming renders any criticism impossible since the fact of blooming is irreducible. This seems to exclude any possibility of "difference." The bloom is irreducible because no possible effort can fully explain it. It may well be inconceivable without effort, but no effort is sufficient to merit or to extort it. Contrasted with the activity of effort, it is an impersonal event. Contrasted with the monstrosities produced by our own efforts, it is a heaven-sent work of art. It is a miracle and a gift. In this respect it is to be compared with artistic inspiration or enthusiasm resulting in something that Plato calls divine and "a find of the Muse." A find is something we do not make ourselves but happen upon, complete and blooming. The same might be said of fruit. "Fruit," says Ruygers, "is a gift. That is to say that it can never be reduced to the forces that produced it, no matter how much activity was involved. The making of a product is bound by rules, fruit is conceived." Bloom is just as much granted as cultivated. One simply accepts the phenomenon, pausing in contemplation. The flowers disarm thought.

But, says Angelus Silesius, the blooming rose does not bloom for whoever chances to see it. This means that contemplation is a disinterested act. We do not annex that which blooms by the fact that we witness it, nor is the blooming expressly intended for the camera of our attention. Just as blooming is a halt at the climax of evolution, its contemplation is also a disinterested pausing. As far as that goes, this is a pleonasm, for contemplation is essentially disinterested. This very fact makes it the fitting method of approach toward that which is blooming and thus distinguishes it from every other form of thought or calculation.

There are two aspects to this detachment, depending on whether it is viewed from the object contemplated or from contemplation itself. According to the way in which it approaches its object, contemplation is a manner of thought that excludes any plan or intention with regard to the object. In other words, contemplation is thought that aspires to no practical consequences. It does not want to do anything with or make anything of its object. It cannot in any case, for a thing in bloom is everything already, even though, biologically speaking, it must be viewed as a preliminary stage. Youth too is a preliminary phase, but the way in which it asserts itself is absoluteness itself. Lichtenberg, of whom Goethe observes that each of his witty remarks poses a problem, says of it: "The blossom is followed by the unripe fruit, but the blossom is in itself a perfection. So too with man. The teenager is considered more perfect than the man of thirty or forty. Only then comes another period of completion, maturity."

Contemplation is the form of thought that allows the thing to be what it is at that moment. It is an uncritical, lyrical observation. It is a seeing and only a seeing, with an eye made aware. The contemplative eye does not touch things but leaves them as they are. If the rose blooms because it blooms, the eye desires only to witness this without intervening in the identity of the rose with itself, without anticipating fruit, maturity, and seed. Contemplation thus is a one-sided seeing, not reciprocal, a frontier situation in thought and observation that man can allow himself only with regard to things and not his fellow men. With regard to youth, as described above, it is ethically and pedagogically unjustifiable. Anyone who takes youth so absolutely, giving it the chance to behave as the norm of human life, not only betrays human maturity but also proclaims that he does not in fact take youth seriously. He is trying to run with the hares and hunt with the hounds.

Contemplation is not reciprocal, not for any lack of will or desire but simply because reciprocity does not enter into the matter. It is of necessity a sublimated form of spying in which one is a surprised but uninvited witness. The contemplative eye is not a gaze that finds response, for the blossom on which it rests is, in its identity with itself, incapable of any response. Every response and every dialogue take place in the deferment of identity; pure identity is blind and dumb. The bloom has even no eye for itself; the rose "achtet nicht ihrer selbst, fragt nicht ob man sie sieht." Flowers do not draw attention to themselves and have no knowledge of contemplation.

Contemplation thus is the method of approach that poses absolutely no questions of whatever it approaches. Here we see revealed a second aspect of its detachment, the detachment of actual contemplation. As a means of thought, contemplation is also a pausing. It is not a progressive but a pausing thinking that not only has no designs on its object but even has no designs on itself. It has no practical intentions, nor has it any theoretical intentions either. It is thought without logic and without conclusions.

The *cogito* of the rose is a *cogito* without *ergo* or, to put it more accurately, the contemplation of the blooming rose is a *cogito* without *ergo*. In this respect too it is only a seeing, as the word itself says clearly enough. The *cogito, ergo sum* is not disinterested. It desires to be a foundation and a cornerstone. The *cogito* of the person contemplating is identical with the *cogito* of the rose in which it loses itself. Bertus Aafjes expresses this idea in his *Voetreis naar Rome*. He calls roses the "soft femininity of nature" and speaks in this connection of the "deep awareness that I exist." Here the rose reaches beyond itself:

> You are rooted deeper in my life
>   than any passing bloom,
> You are written in my heart,
>   pure *cogito, ergo sum.*

And he continues,

> For my existence would
>   lose all meaning
> Without the magic of the rose.

2. *Causality and Contemplation*

The contemplation of the rose in bloom is a frontier situation in thought, a fleeting moment that cannot be considered a norm for thinking behavior. As part of the mystique of identity it ignores deferment but it is an authentic form of thought insofar as it is not alienated from wonder. In the identity of the blossom, wonder attains its end term without becoming alienated from itself since it excludes any form of explanation. This exclusion keeps deferment open and wonder alive. Thought can never see beyond wonder, and explanation puts an end to wonder. Just as one can imagine a trivial and a divine identity, one can also conceive of a thought before and after wonder which is not inspired by wonder.

Hegel, whose system has an answer for everything, including wonder, says of it:

> The man who as yet wonders at nothing, lives on in dull obtuseness. Nothing interests him and nothing exists for him since he has not yet succeeded in detaching himself from objects and their immediate singular existence. But he, on the other hand, who no longer wonders at anything, who regards the whole of the external world as

something which he has thrashed out for himself, either in the abstract-rational manner of a general human development or in the noble and deeper consciousness of absolute mental freedom and universality, has attained insight and has thus changed objects and their existence by his mental and self-aware insight into them. Wonder, on the contrary, exists only where man, having torn himself loose from the most direct and primary attachments to nature and from the most primary, purely practical attachment of his desire, dissociates himself mentally from nature and seeks in things something general, which exists of itself and is permanent. Only then does he observe the things in nature; they are something different which nonetheless must exist for him and in which he tries to rediscover himself, thought, reason. For the suspicion of something higher and the awareness of something outside himself is still indistinct while yet a contrast exists between natural things and the mind to which things owe their attractive as well as their repulsive effect. It is precisely the experience of this contradiction and the urge to surmount it that incites wonder.

The first product of this situation is that on the one hand man imagines nature and objective existence in general as a ground outside himself and venerates it as a power while at the same time satisfying his need to imagine as external his subjective feeling of something higher, subjective, general and to contemplate it as objective.

This is what Hegel has to say on wonder.

He describes it further as a disquiet, but for him it is not a principle but rather a beginning which must be surmounted. One of the ways of surmounting this disquiet is that of causal thinking. One of the prime seductions of thought is indeed to plunge into causal connections and series, thereby becoming serious and acquiring scientific pretensions. It is not for nothing that one of the basic rules of thought is: *nil fit sine ratione,* "nothing is done without cause." The fact that Leibniz was the first to put it into words does not mean that it did not operate before his time but does perhaps signify the beginning of a deliberate rationalism, the pretension that this identity of being and thought which occurs in ratio in the double meaning of "ground" and "reason" can also be attained and formulated so that thought can lead to scientific certainty.

The principle may contain some degree of truth but it does not necessarily follow that the reason for every phenomenon can pin down or establish its ratio. For thought inspired by wonder the ground proves an abyss. The identity of ratio as reason and ratio as basis, of account and causality, is a deferred identity, and as long as philosophy dwells in deferment it experiences identity as nonidentity and ground as abyss. Abyss is ground in its nonidentity. Wonder sets causal thought in motion by the principle of establishing a ground but suspends it again at the prospect of the unending series that thereby rises up. The "thusness" of things is rooted in the particular effect of a cause, but that particular effect is, in itself and as mobility, an expression of nonidentity and again requires another cause.

It is an endless chain. This endlessness is more the object of philosophical thought than would be the task of halting the series by establishing a first cause, as Aristotle does in accepting a *primum movens immobile*. To do this is roughly the same as attributing an independent existence to ideas and attempting to draw up an exact basis and calculation with them. It may be a basic truth, but a basic truth is one from which no conclusion can be drawn, precisely because it is the end and, as the end, cannot be located in a clear series but disappears beyond the horizon. A fundamental truth cannot be founded, just as the standard measure cannot be measured nor the standard weight weighed.

The contemplation of a causal series is in fact a perception of nonidentity. The fact that everything has a ground means that everything is different, that the "other" is revealed in the like and that they are radically connected. The thing has a cause; thing and cause are related as like and other. Causality thus is one of the names given, from the viewpoint of wonder, to the refractory link between things and within the thing itself. It is a law of thought, but it is no concern of philosophical thought to follow all the ways of applying this law. Its concern is to radicalize the wonder it arouses.

Thought is a victory over force and immediate identification. Force does not tolerate the deferment of identity. Thought, on the contrary, is the slowness in which deferment is borne and endured. But the causal explanation which "gives" things a clear identity is a subtle form of force. It cannot thus be the goal of thought to explain things. It would become alienated from itself in the endless series of causal explanations and might degenerate into force. It remains radically floating and hanging in the contemplation of infinity in which it is still wonder.

3. *Occasionalism and Wonder*

This seems a strange attitude, but force does not always immediately mean war. It can also be directed against appearances and, according to an old formula, it is philosophy's task to save appearances, which is not the same thing as explaining them. One might conceive of a very pious form of force that applies the *primum movens immobile* on every occasion when it cannot provide an explanation. If we call that *movens immobile* god, it is clear that a causal explanation which has direct recourse to god is a form of force with regard to every other explanation.

A most edifying and profound example of this is the so-called occasionalism of Geulincx and Malebranche, two philosophers of the school of Descartes. The latter had already been obliged to fall back upon god and divine qualities to provide a basis for the human knowledge of his *cogito*. For if the higher being is deceptive that *cogito* has no value. Once this knowledge is set in motion as an endless series a domain is roped off in which the human arbitrary will can know and explain completely and mechanically as a pure extension. There is a clear and constituted dualism of knowledge and expansion, soul and body which is much more rigorous than with the Greek

Plato. No mutual influence of soul and body is thus possible. They are two worlds, each with its own order, between which no communication is possible.

There is here an absolute dualism which attributes a separate identity to opposite poles. Anyone who clings to this notion embarks upon a series of reasonings in order to explain how it is possible that certain phenomena appear to occur at the same time in soul and body, how the mental will, for instance, can cause an arm or leg to move. Since this dualism here is much more serious than with Plato and is linked with fanatically professed religious views, the reasoning lacks the mythical character and playful tone with which Plato speaks of preexistence, anamnesis, immortality, and of the body as the prison of the soul. We are dealing here with causal reasonings with scientific pretensions.

When now it is granted on the one hand that soul and body cannot influence each other while yet it cannot be denied that certain frequently occurring phenomena in human behavior indicate at least a simultaneous influence, the next step, in order to save appearances, not to have to deny them, is obviously to fall back on a miracle. This miracle would be performed every time by god himself on the occasion of an impulse to movement in a soul that is itself powerless. On the occasion of that impulse, the prime mover moves the body, and this reasoning is called by philosophers occasionalism. The same can be said of knowledge as of movement. "God employs the physical process, e.g. the effect of stimuli on the senses, in order to bring about the appropriate process in the soul, perception." In Geulincx's opinion human, ethical activity is not possible without this conclusive, causal explanation of knowledge. *Quod nescis quomodo facis, id non facis,* "if we do not know how to do a thing, then we do not do it." We might say that we ourselves do not do and know but that we receive the knowledge from god and that we move in him. We cannot be said to do but to be done to. This is not only a pious theory but an archaic concept.

Augustine too shows himself to be a member of the classical world with his theory of divine illumination in human knowledge. Classical life moves in a parallelism between human and cosmic life. One of its important aspects is a belief in the decisive influence of moon and stars on human life. This parallelism is an infinite deferment of the coincidence of identity. It creates space for an event in which humanity plays no part, space in which man can breathe and in which he can raise his arms to heaven to implore an intervention that he is incapable of achieving. This freedom is the reverse of fatalism. In this deferment they are identical or, at least, the contradiction between them is rendered less oppressive. This is what makes the belief in moon and stars, the confidence in the influence of the endless distance, so enviable.

With Homer it is not man who thinks. The god who appears to him inspires him just as the muse the poet. We refer literally here to an archaic concept, not from pure verbalism but out of wonder. For the archaic parallelism, occasionalism, and the related concept by Leibniz of a *harmonia praestabilita* can all be traced back to wonder at the mighty thing that took place in human activity, at the result that surpasses the effort, the fruit that is a gift, the flower that is a pausing.

But this must be done without the scientific pretension of hereby explaining a miracle. A miracle is that which cannot be explained, provided always that it is kept outside causal reasoning. Once it becomes involved in this, the miracle is no more than a troublesome relic, a stumbling block to man's independent powers of reasoning. The miracle exists, not as an unexplainable relic but as that which makes causal thought impossible; it incites to wonder. But I can very well wonder at the movement of my arm or at my knowledge without wishing to explain this movement or this knowledge neatly, with no loose ends attached. This indeed is authentic wonder. As soon as I start looking for causal explanations off my own bat or start crying miracle or, what amounts to the same thing, fall back on a direct intervention by god, I am dealing in pseudo-explanations and pseudo-philosophy.

The authentic character of occasionalism is not so much the series of reasonings on which it is based as the contemplation of a wondrous happening, each explanation of which should of itself express wonder, nothing more. It is a splendid concept in which the self-evident becomes a miracle with no feeling of force, provided the word god here is not interpreted too rigorously but, for instance, as a sign of "the other." If god is used to do away with wonder and to introduce a new, almost juridically determined matter-of-factness, he is deformed into an idol. The man who marvels at the wonders of life and, because of this sense of wonder, refuses to use god as a direct explanation but, as it were, persists in the desperation of his wonder without wishing to appropriate god is probably more pious and more religious than the man who fabricates a god to explain the unexplainable; for once his god has obliged, he is given his marching orders.

Apart from this rigorous, dogmatic viewpoint, which might be regarded as a religious determinism with aspirations to distant physiological domains, the word *occasio* as chance, opportunity, or moment, might serve to indicate the link between doing and happening better than *causa*, which seems to want to provide too neat an explanation. *Occasio* leaves both independence and happening freer than *causa*. It is less pretentious to say that the act is the *occasio* of the event than that it is the *causa*. And what is less pretentious with regard to an object of wonder—such as the link between doing and happening—is more correct. The *occasio* does not impose the link but gives it a chance. We tend to act more occasionally than causally. *Occasio* leaves action more freedom, even in the sense that every act might be motivated by just one *causa* but by more than one *occasio*.

Nine

WONDER AND SURPRISE

1. The Gift

To persist in wonder at the existence of miracles and gifts means to live in a state of gratitude that cannot be addressed statically to a giver. This inability to show gratitude probably contributed in no small measure to the development of a certain concept, such as fear, that was used from time immemorial to explain the gods. It is almost impossible to think of a gift without at the same time imagining a giver. An anonymous gift is scarcely a gift at all. Yet gratitude must come to terms with this nonidentity of the gift. Even though the giver is anonymous and unattainable, this is no reason for saying that he does not exist. In any case the experience of being as a gift can make itself irresistibly felt in wonder. Heidegger, as we have seen, speaks of being as giving and thought as thanking.

A gift is given and received. There are a giver, a receiver, and a gift. These three are indispensable in the rhythm of giving and taking.

In the first place the gift is given. There is someone who

gives it. It is not found or taken by force. It is not entirely anonymous nor is it a product of the person who receives it. It is proffered by another or the other and accepted within the like. Here "the other" is the extreme limit to which anonymity can go. The verb "to give" is linked etymologically with words that mean "take" or "grasp" and with the Latin *habere* in the sense of "to keep." To give seems to mean to hold out, offer, *prae-habere*, *praebere*. To give is to offer, to hold out invitingly. The giver places the gift in the space between himself and the other. There is no compulsion attached. The giver does not hold the gift tightly in front of him so that attention is drawn more to him than to the gift. As giver, he retires at arms' length. Pious spirits will say that god, the greatest giver, retreats the farthest, indeed so far that he is no longer seen or recognized as giver. This is one of the finest conceivable "proofs" of the existence of God but it may also result in his being unrecognized and remaining anonymous.

The other can accept what is offered to him or he can refuse it. It is not flung at him in such a way that he can do nothing but catch it. There is no arbitrary element in giving. The giver does not demand gratitude or even that his gift should be accepted. Anyone who demands gratitude is a bad giver. To offer means that the giver brings his gift and the hand with which he intends to give it into proximity with the intended recipient, but there is no compulsion attached. The gift is in a floating state between someone who no longer has it and someone who has not yet got it. It is here that it matures into a gift.

This then is the situation of giving. The gesture of giving a gift is never a careless flinging but a careful accompaniment. The giver of the gift is present by the giving and in the gift, not outside it. He transfers himself to the other in and with the gift. In Dutch, the word *schenken*, "to give or confer a gift," also means "to pour," and is associated with words like "sloping" and "tilted." *Schenken* is a causative verb meaning "to tilt." The word derives from a situation in which a man gives another man or an animal a drink. *Schenken* is to tilt the bucket or jar so that the liquid inside can flow out into mouth or cup. The *geschenk,* or "gift," is that which is poured out in this manner, the drink which is offered.

The gift then is fluid, liquid, and thirst quenching. It is transferred carefully between one and the other. This thirst must be understood symbolically. It is a real need to which "giving" or "pouring" corresponds as an answer. The reply is a gift in the context of the question which expresses a structured expectation. Expectation means getting ready to receive the gift, and thus is not an arbitrary construction. The gift is not that which is asked for and expected. Still less is it the contrary, for the more concrete my expectation the less receptive I am to the contrary and the less willing to accept it as a gift. The gift corresponds to my receptivity, my thirst, my expectation but in such a way that it is for me a surprise and a wonder.

The surprise is the wonder at the gift; this wonder is so elementary that it has been given a separate name in which the "thusness" of the gift is contrasted to the "other-ness" of the expectation. Although the gift is awaited with a feeling of receptiveness, it is nonetheless a surprise. Expectation therefore cannot be qualified as an urgent need. There are no obligations attached to the gift. An obligatory gift is almost an impossibility; this explains why it is more difficult to give a person a gift on his birthday or at Christmas than on a day that has no particular significance, when his expectation is reduced to a minimum form of receptivity with no strings attached. This is why, at the fixed and ritually prescribed giving times, we tend rather to seek a gift substitute whereby the obligation is met, as it were, in a pitiful sort of humor.

Receptivity and expectation do not ask, demand, or earn the gift; it cannot be determined from the viewpoint of expectation. Expectation allows the giver full freedom, and this freedom in its turn is determined by the expectation. Whatever is quite contrary to expectation cannot be called a gift since it gives surprise no opportunity to find an outlet in gratitude. I cannot give a baby in the cradle a bicycle as a gift; it would not reach its destination. I hold it in my offering hand but he does not accept it. The gift does not acquire its liquidity whereby it becomes a gift in the space between giver and recipient. Still less can I give an old man a rattle and delude myself that I am giving him a gift. A relationship does exist thus between gift and expectation or receptivity but, within certain limits, it carries no obligations.

There are other limits to giving, determined by the nature of the gift itself. The gift is not only a gesture but, in the hand making the gesture, something is offered. The gift is, no matter how, that which is given. The value of the gift is determined not only by the gesture with which the giver offers himself in his gift at the proper moment but also by the nature of the thing he gives. The attention with which one man turns to another is not yet a gift, even though we speak of "paying attention." The value of a gift is determined also by its content. Not everything becomes a gift by the fact of being given, which may be said to entitle the present industry to a certain right of existence. An old newspaper is not a gift. It might become a gift for some particular person, but in this case it would not be just any old newspaper.

A thing becomes a gift only in concert with receptivity, the expectation of the person receiving it. A gift is valuable when it would have meaning for the recipient, even as an anonymous find. Giving must also satisfy this condition. A thing does not derive its value as a gift from its meaning as a gesture, nor from the significance it holds for the actual giver. When a child offers me a drawing, thus establishing very personal contact with me, I can appreciate the gesture without regarding the drawing as a gift. For that which has meaning and value for the child is not necessarily meaningful to me, even after this contact.

It is not essential that the gift should hold great significance for the giver himself, that it should be a painful wrench for him to part with it. This would be an arbitrary

action, placing too much emphasis on the giver. It is sufficient that his gesture should express a realization that
what he gives has meaning for the other. What I give
becomes dear to me through the receptivity of the other.
A gift that remains completely worthless to the giver after
it has changed hands is just as unreal as one that has no
meaning for the recipient. Whoever gives, always gives
himself, says Gabriel Marcel.

Yet the value that the gift possesses for the giver is not
"gift value" if it is not also determined by the receptivity
of the recipient. This is not always understood, and there
are various interpretations of gift, sacrifice, and suitability
for sacrifice that fail to take this into account. The idea
already emerges in the sixth book of the *Iliad* that a
sacrifice to the divinity acquires value in proportion to its
worth to the person making the sacrifice, that it will have
a more powerful magical effect when it is, as it were, carved
out of one's own substance. Hector orders his mother to
sacrifice to Athena the finest garment she has and the
one she is most fond of. Here, probably under pressure of
emergency, one particular aspect of the gift is declared to
be its essence. The gesture is intensified in a magical
manner to insure a better reception. Man sacrifices part of
himself in order to establish a more probable claim to what
he keeps. Anyone who measures the value of a gift by its
significance for himself takes too little account of the other
to be really called a giver. This is forgivable in children
but, for this very reason, their gifts are not yet authentic.

The gift thus is not asked for, nor is it expected in any
concrete and determined fashion, yet it holds a significance
for the recipient since it anticipates his wish. It anticipates
a desire which the recipient was not yet aware of as a
clearly defined need but which did exist in him and is now
given concrete form by the gift. A gift is always something
that the recipient is glad to possess. It gives rise to the
wish and fulfills it at the same time. It identifies
the wish with himself and thus confirms the recipient
in his individuality.

Since it is something the recipient is glad to possess, the gift has a surplus meaning, its desirability at the precise moment it is given. This moment—the meeting between giver and recipient at which the giver, in agreement with the recipient, makes an *acte de presence* in the thing and then retires—gives the thing that surplus quality which transforms it into a gift or a favor. Only by this can gratitude be aroused. I am not grateful for what I have taken or earned or for what has been flung at me. Gratitude is a sense of joy directed toward its cause, the other. It cannot be an obligation. Spinoza says that only free men can be grateful to each other.

2. *Thanks and Praise*

Since gratitude is focused on the other its identity is not yet completely determined. For in his "otherness" the other remains the nonidentified. This too allows gratitude its freedom. It is no more susceptible to compulsion than are wonder and surprise, enthusiasm and happiness. It is no ethical obligation to be fulfilled without deferment; indeed its place is within an unending deferment. It is no merit to regard being as a gift, but our good fortune or happiness. This happiness is not causally related to human independence nor is it a product of it. Happiness cannot be explained causally, just as it eludes those who pursue it most purposefully. The person who, having received it as a gift, wishes afterward to situate it in a causal series is simply doing an injustice to happiness and enthusiasm. Gratitude for the gift of being can never find an adequate and definitive outlet, not even in the concept of god. Thought as thanks must renounce the construction of causal series and be willing to face up to its own desperation. It pauses in an unending openness and focuses upon it. This openness itself is the space and temple of contemplation.

It is this that completely distinguishes gratitude as an ethical attitude inspired by wonder from gratitude as a feudal obligation of slave to master. There is also a clear distinction in ethical quality; a gift given with the intention of compelling gratitude ceases to be a gift. Gratitude felt as an obligation turns the giver into a tyrannical master. Only when they renounce this rapid identification can each be thought of as adequate. Gratitude can only avoid slavery by focusing tentatively on an anonymous giver rather than addressing itself to a clearly conceived creator who is bound to his identity. Under the same conditions being can be experienced as a real gift, a favor that leaves the favored one free and does not demand a deliberate return in exchange.

A gift is more purely a gift in proportion to the freedom it leaves to the recipient, even in the matter of expressing gratitude. Because the giver remains the other and retreats into anonymity, no master-slave relationship develops nor is there any question of mutual barter. There is no room here for the constricting feeling that something is expected of us in return, a feeling that can inspire ingratitude and even hostility toward the giver. We are better able to enjoy a favor and to accept it as such when the giver of that favor is himself prepared to forget it and to disassociate himself from it. The gift that inspires most gratitude is not that which puts us under most obligation but that which is given best.

Anyone who is able to regard the being of things as the gift of a creator will also praise the creator for not imposing himself and his kindness in his gift. He cannot at the same time insist on gratitude toward this creator, for if creation is a gift it is a perfectly given gift. Creation as a gift is thus a dubious proof of God's existence, for it is precisely as a gift that it proves the absence and anonymity of the giver. A theology of the *deus absconditus*, which proclaims hiddenness as God's proper mode of existence, should be content to leave it at this statement. This declaration derives its value solely from the fact that it is gratuitous. Only gratuitous assertions can be made about *gratia*. The gift does not impose the giver. If he is already felt to be present in it, this also means that he withdraws outside in absence and anonymity so that his actual existence is no longer relevant.

This idea can be developed from the theological point of view. Dorothee Sölle does so to a certain extent in her book *Christ the Representative*. It might also be elaborated psychologically and therapeutically in the sense that ideal therapy is not regarded as a causal change brought about by an other. The patient in this case changes only within himself, the essential factor of this process being that he is not made to feel that he has become a different person from one day to the next as the result of an abrupt and startling miracle. A shock such as this can only be absorbed by thought and it is the registration of this shock that constitutes thought. It is the function of thought to radicalize and to generalize this shock. It is not its function to pump it into the blood as excitement and neurosis as is done in the error of haste and in the requirement of gratitude as prostration before a clearly recognizable giver. Such a requirement is an intellectual error and a form of moral compulsion.

There is too much short-sighted moralization about gratitude from a self-righteous and impatient standpoint which tolerates no deferment at all. Impatience leads us to regard gratitude as a heavy obligation which we subsequently and with heroic effort attempt to elevate again above our own interest, the only factor that might make gratitude possible at this banal level. In doing this we are using the infinite deferment for our own ends. It was this sort of gratitude that Kant had in mind—and he knew little of human nature. "Gratitude is duty, that is to say not simply a maxim for crafty behavior whereby, by giving proof of my recognition for favors received, I hope to move the other to still greater benefits." Such a view of gratitude is an arid, listless despair, an attempt by means of a powerful effort of will to reach beyond an endless indefinable deferment. It is, thus, excessively egotistical as well as being an act of force.

Such a view is probably associated with feudal social relationships in which abject gratitude toward stern governors and patrons was indeed a means of eliciting greater favors. It assumes a constituted distinction between master and servant which admits of no reciprocity. One is by definition always the giver and one the recipient. The harsh obligation of gratitude can only develop in this senseless fossilization of identities. In these conditions the ethical quality of this obligation can only be a denial of precisely those circumstances which serve to perpetuate it. If I have to be grateful to the master, purely and simply grateful, even apart from his favors, then this favor will continue to be guaranteed as a favor and caprice, and the slave will be always at the mercy of this caprice. If the beggar has to be grateful for alms, the social injustice that made him a beggar can continue to exist. "In this way," says Plattel, "this giving becomes a refined attack on that which is most unique and sacred in man: his freedom."

The same feudal source may have given rise to the bitterness at man's ingratitude which has inspired so much cynical worldly wisdom. Once again it is not the servant or the beggar who complains of ingratitude or, in the rare comedies in which this does occur, it is at best a wary humor. The person who complains bitterly of ingratitude is the same person who expects and demands prompt gratitude, thus attributing to himself the power to scatter favors. The person who is so emphatic about conferring favors turns himself into a petty, tyrannical, bad, and cruel imitation of the creator. He invites ungratefulness and revolt for, says Nietzsche, "heavy obligations do not arouse gratitude but vengeance and if the small benefit is not forgotten there grows from it a gnawing worm." We can obtain a pure view of gratitude only when the favor received is a gift with no strings attached, when it is a surplus and does not replace something to which a person is entitled. In this way we can obtain a clear and undistracted view of the actual thing given. Gratitude is joy on account of things and what things are. It is ethically wrong to try to slot gratitude into a causally founded series that leads to the logical conclusion that gratitude should be a duty. Gratitude has no rational "because" but a free "in spite of."

Greek has one word for thanks, favor, and for the gift-character of the thing: *charis*. *Charis* is charm, favor, and thanks, just like the Latin *gratia* which in Christian Latin has the additional meaning of "grace." These words express favor as a free granting, without jealousy or the obligation to offer something in return. The thing is something accepted with delight. Thanks is a reflection of the glow from that which is granted as a favor. *Charis* is the surplus that the thing acquires as gift, fruit and blossom, and expresses both giving and receiving together and in equal measure. Here gratitude and praise can develop since they are not subjected to pressure but are given their proper space in which to unfold.

Praise can become a literary and philosophical form, eulogy a genre. Originally praise was an expression of gratitude, a poetical confirmation of man's surprise at the gift of things. Praise is addressed to the gift, to the being of things, and to the great happening in which expectation is surpassed. From time immemorial poetry is praising, giving space to things, elevating them to a level at which they cannot be passed or forgotten, recognizing the surplus to which they can lay claim on the grounds or abyss of their gift-character. As a philosophical principle praise could be an attempt to attribute a maximal significance to things. As such it has occasionally been abused by sophists as an apologia for the worthless, an exercise in quibbling. The eulogy is most abused, however, by servile spirits seeking to extort fresh favors from their master.

3. *Acceptance and Feast*

To receive a thing as a favor is to accept it in a festive manner. There is nothing matter-of-fact about this acceptance. The surprise must be capable of being absorbed and not seek an outlet prematurely; an endless deferment must be endured. The acceptance of gratuitous existence assumes the capacity for great passivity. Experience of life is essential for a feast. What we call the art of feasting is not a meaningful concept for people below a certain age. They think that perhaps it is something that can be learned from a book. Yet this art cannot be learned from any book, unless it is the book of life.

The art of feasting begins when one has read sufficiently in the book of life. It has been said that life begins at forty. This is not only a great consolation for those on the wrong side of thirty; so far as the art of feasting is concerned, it is also a clearly discernible fact. Children and very young people simply cannot feast, for a feast is more concerned with the fruits of life than with its blossom. For young people a feast is not yet a feast but, at the very best, a party —and that is something quite different. It is not even a small feast or the shadow of a feast. A party differs from a feast just as radically as a soap bubble from a balloon or lemonade from brandy. In any case, party is only a slight word without a clear etymology which in itself is significant enough. A party is just a little bit more than nothing but still almost too little for a real word.

Teenagers hold parties, people celebrate feasts. Teenagers and children are bad at celebrating feasts. The festive atmosphere can be completely ruined by the presence of too many teenagers. In cafes the eruption of such a gang of screaming youngsters brings an immediate feeling of unease. They are too young to understand the art of feasting and too obstinate to realize the fact. They bring with them something that the others have already left behind and exploit it to the utmost. There is nothing festive about their superficiality since it has nothing to set it off.

A feast is the product of the totality of life, and the very young do not know enough about life to make a feast out of the same material from which life is woven. This material does not consist solely of a zest for life. That is only the warp. Melancholy, dissatisfaction with life is the woof. The whole of life is not present in a party since there is no melancholy to be surmounted. A party is a foaming, superficial phenomenon, fine and sparkling perhaps, but lacking the bottomless abyss. It lacks a dimension that

the feast possesses and that is directly linked with melancholy, the dregs of life. A beaming, cheerful face is no
guarantee of festive joy no matter how much pleasure
it radiates.

Older people may envy that pleasure, and it may be
fortunate for children that they are not yet able to feast,
but no one whose life has already begun and for whom
things can sometimes crowd so festively together would
want to return to this situation. Our jealousy with regard
to very young people contains an element of sympathy,
the same sympathy we show toward the people in the cave
and people who are tyrannized. Young people suffer the
tyranny of thinking they know it all.

With all this we have not defined exactly what a feast is
nor what the art of feasting consists of. This would be
impossible anyway since it would rivet the feast to its own
identity. There are, however, a few words we can ponder
on, for instance, the word "solemn" and the expression "to
celebrate a feast." A feast is celebrated; that is the fixed
expression for it. At a feast we also give rein to our joy
or our desires. Here another element is introduced. In
Dutch the "rein" is the thin rope on which you fly a kite.
To give rein to the kite is to give it a longer piece of rope
to allow it to rise higher. The kite's ascent is its conquest
of space. One pays out the rope, the line to which a thing
is attached, in order to allow it a greater expansion. To give
rein to one's desires is to give them the opportunity to
develop more freely and to occupy the space to which they
lay claim, to loosen the ties that bind them, to allow them
more freedom. To give rein to desires is to allow them to
be what they are. Lack of freedom deformed or decapitated
those desires. They did not show their true nature. Now
their own shape is restored to them.

"To celebrate" can also have the meaning of "to respect"
or "to spare." To celebrate someone is to cause him no
trouble, to leave him in his being. We celebrate a person
because we rely upon the development of that being or
because we wish to spare him a tiresome conformism. We
relieve him of certain obligations that continue to be bind-

ing for others. These obligations may change into pleasure. A celebrated person is someone we look up to, whom we allow to develop his own character. The banquets and toasting take second place. This emerges in the expression "celebrated orator." However, "to celebrate" is something quite different from "to make much of" or else we should have to prove that "making much of" is also a celebration in the sense of "looking up to." In any case, it is a fact that the celebrated person, looked up to or made much of, is allowed more freedom than another, and is less restricted by life in the cave. He is allowed to be himself, we confer on him the rare boon of granting him his nature or essence.

Is it necessary to know what constitutes the essence of a feast in order to understand what the expression "to feast" means, or to take part in a feast ourselves? Or is it possible to celebrate that still unknown essence and to let it loose in its own space? It is indeed, for feasting does not create the essence; it only creates the space for it. One leaves in its essence that which is autonomous, which already possesses its own existence. One approves of that existence and allows it to develop according to its own pattern of disposition and possibilities.

Celebrating a feast is therefore something quite different from organizing one. An organizer attempts to lead an occurrence into clearly defined paths that he himself has drawn out and thus to keep it completely under control. Celebrating, however, means providing space for a development, the dimensions of which cannot yet be anticipated. In a certain sense, it must be said that it is part of the as-yet-unknown nature of the feast that the feaster's attitude should be somewhat passive. It does not depend on us whether or not the feast is a success. Organization can outline a pattern but it is not this that makes the feast.

To celebrate a feast is to allow the feast to develop according to its nature, and the first thing we should know about this nature is that it is the autonomy of the actual feast; this also consists of the fact that the feast has its own nature. Such a gaggle of tautologies can only lead to the conclusion that a feast can be nothing else than a feast and cannot be turned into a feast by anything but a feast. I can of course give a festive dinner to enhance my status a little or to sweeten the relations, but the more ulterior motives I have the deeper the autonomous nature of the feast is buried under a crust of unfestiveness. It has less space to develop and there is more likelihood that it will degenerate into a party or be a complete write-off. Strictly speaking it is even impossible to isolate any festive occurrence that gives the feast its character, for the feast already possesses this character.

The festive event can be nothing more than the occasion that brings the feasters together and sets the feast going. As soon as the feast has got properly started the occasion for it tends to be increasingly forgotten and rejected by the feast's organism as a foreign body. The person responsible for the feast becomes the "guest of honor," sacrificed by the revelers to the autonomous feast. To celebrate a feast is to allow it to take its own course. And this course is decided not by the person giving the feast nor by those attending it but by the feast itself. Now it might occur to me to wonder how a feast manages this, since it is no divine power capable of deciding anything. This may be so but it is equally true that none of the revelers is responsible for the feast. I cannot state how this occurs; in any case it is not our concern but the concern of the feast itself which makes its own laws. The art of celebrating a feast consists simply of obeying those laws.

It may be objected that if this is so there is a considerable danger that the feast will degenerate. Anyone who allows a feast to take its course and does not keep it within bounds is left to pick up the pieces, materially and morally. This is a risk that has to be taken. It would be interesting to know whether this risk increases or diminishes the more we face up to it. In my opinion it is impossible to celebrate a feast without taking this risk, and it belongs to the nature of the feast to opt for the positive side of life while a morality which draws up its own rules will tend to tug it toward the negative side. In any case no feast can flourish without a margin of freedom. To put it even more strongly this freedom extends to the limits of transgression, to dissipation. "A feast," says Freud, "is the solemn transgression of a commandment." Freud thinks that the festive mood is aroused by the liberation of what is otherwise forbidden, but rather the reverse is true. But then it is difficult to explain where this festive mood comes from. However we should not attempt to explain a gift. The essential things in life fall from heaven and remain floating just above any possible basis of explanation. Let us rather say that out of an obscure impulse of joie de vivre and melancholy, experienced together as a climax in life, is born a mood that we call the festive mood and in which we enjoy total freedom.

The morality of arbitrariness and force, impatience and tyranny, becomes liquid and transparent in the light of the gift. Then we say things that we would otherwise find difficult to express and we say them to people of whom we are ordinarily afraid. We do things that tend just to exceed our usual measure of playfulness. The feudal framework is breached at a feast: all are equal. There are no superiors or inferiors, no givers or receivers. This equality can of itself be celebrated as a feast in which the superiors serve their inferiors or the children are given the run of the house, but basically this is just another effect of the feast. The same can be said of all forms of excess such as extravagance, drunkennes, outspokenness, and license. These are products of the feast that confirm and emphasize its nature. The emphasis of the feast can reach its climax in intoxication or in an orgy, and in many a middle-class feast the procession through the house is the decent, ritual replacement of this climax. Indeed it quite frequently occurs that more or less natural excesses are replaced by rituals that remain within the laws of the feast. Their purpose is to serve freedom and license.

During a Roman triumph the celebrated imperator was not only honored but also mocked in a manner that would not be tolerated today. The person in whose honor the feast is given is degraded to the status of boor because the feast must be able to take its own course without being dominated by anyone or linked to too premature an identity. A component part of certain Greek religious feasts was called "aeschrology." On such occasions, according to Van der Leeuw, elegant and extremely respectable matrons had to tell jokes of a more or less obscene character. This aeschrology too is a festive excess but kept within ritual bounds.

This keeping within bounds will also have belonged to the laws of the feast. The feasters were experimenting with a freedom that they did not fully and at once comprehend. The feast is celebrated, but celebrated solemnly. This quality of solemnity is the beginning of the festive and its emphasis invests it with a unique order. It is the emphasis that attaches to particular moments of life. The feast is the highest positive experience of life. The words "solemn" and "duty" are inevitably linked, and both convey the idea of doing a thing with emphasis. Duty is a deed performed with great emphasis and deliberation. To act solemnly is to act in such a way that the performance of the action incorporates a contemplation of its meaning, thus acquiring a contemplative character. Its aim is not, as with a banal action, to attain a desired effect as quickly as possible; it rejoices in its own course.

This is what, from the very beginning, raises the feast, solemnly begun, above the level of daily life. No matter how happy life may be, it cannot be a perpetual feast. The feast, indeed, solemnly and emphatically dissociates itself from that ordinary life with its force and impatience. It wants to be a climax in or rather above that life. It wishes to experience and compress the time in which life takes a special course. The feast is also a revolt against ordinary life, an expression of the awareness that everyday life does not attain its proper level. In the feast, man solemnly detaches himself from the banality of everyday life to which he is riveted and aims at a higher, broader level of humanity which lies above him but which does more justice to the totality of his possibilities, a level at which he should have the right to dwell permanently.

This awareness is also expressed by festive clothing,

for there is no proper feast without it. Garment is already a more festive word than clothing. Festive clothing helps to express the distance from the everyday and the banal and, remarkably enough, creates this distance. This is also the significance of the Sunday suit. By putting on a different suit we adopt another role, we show our willingness to allow expression to other possibilities of our existence. Festive clothing helps us to persist in the solemn and to experience the highest level of our lives. It is an expression of our willingness to keep this level in mind. It is thus understandable that in the Gospels one of the guests who appeared at the feast without his festive garment was cast into the exterior darkness where there were weeping and gnashing of teeth.

That is what happens when one mistakes a feast for a party. To appear without festive clothing is to deny the unique, solemn order of the feast. One reveals oneself as an outsider. A person who appears at the feast in his ordinary, everyday garb equates the festive with the everyday, thereby destroying the possibility of the feast. A feast cannot stand up to this criticism. Anyone who behaves like an outsider, even if it is only by his clothing, does not celebrate the feast but paralyzes it. His lack of receptivity puts the damper on everything.

Like wonder and happiness, a feast is vulnerable and defenseless against criticism. It is precisely that which is highest, most invisible, postulated perhaps only on the basis of our need that can most easily be denied without rational grounds for a refutation of this denial. The feast needs believing and receptive feasters to celebrate its fragile and vulnerable nature. The more approval an illusion has, the easier it is to believe in it. In the very narrow margin in which the positive forces of life gain perhaps over the negative, or rather, in which they celebrate their little triumphs in turn, the feeling can sometimes prevail that zest for living has won. The chance of a feast being a substantial occasion is no greater than the width of that margin. This is what makes it a vulnerable affair that cannot be cherished enough.

Ten

ENDURING DEFERMENT

1. Haste

One of the first decisions of wisdom is the decision to suspend definitive judgment on any matter at all. Wisdom becomes philosophy when it radicalizes this decision not from any arbitrary considerations but rather from a sense of impotence. Doubt, wonder, and epoch have this in common, that they recognize the deferment of decision as the basis of thought. This determines their philosophical form, for philosophy's place after all is in this deferment.

The disquiet aroused by wonder in no way resembles haste. Disquiet is the feeling of witnessing an explosion in the identity of things, an idefinite deferment of identification. Haste is the panic revolt against the absurdity of any deferment of identification. One way of making this clear is by taking traffic as an example. The quicker the means of transport the more haste the person using it must have. A pedestrian cannot allow himself as much haste as a car driver and, therefore, he is not in such a hurry. For him distance is not absurd since his mode of locomotion itself is still a dwelling in deferment. Walking creates contact with things passed.

The car driver does not dwell in deferment. He is simply engaged in traveling from one point to another by means of a machine. These points are the only things that count, the road between is pure, absurd distance, deferment hampering identity. The longer the road and the more emphatic the intention of getting from one point to another, the more absurd this distance becomes. The arbitrary way in which the one point is charged with significance and value drains the surrounding space, and the very possibility of rapid transport can render this intention more emphatic and this distance more absurd. Distance and deferment then become things to be done away with and haste an act or mood of force directed against all that lies in "between" and against the "between" itself.

Haste is total lack of interest, for interest means precisely to dwell in between. Haste is the pathos of active, arbitrary people and, as such, is in contrast with wonder, which halts and looks. Haste does not look but, like rage, is blind. This blindness is the closed nature of an arbitrary existence desiring to impose its constructions immediately upon reality. Haste is a form of rage, directed against deferment, intolerant towards nonidentity. From the ethical point of view this phenomenon has the same root as force. Force is a form of activity which excludes any type of passivity and thus any tolerance, any patience. Just as patience is the culture of passivity, haste is the culture of activity. It is a desperate revolt on the part of active, arbitrary man against deferment as experienced in time. Time is our way of experiencing the deferment of identity, a non-simultaneous granting of possibilities that belong together. In this way haste is related to boredom which emphasizes and renders intolerable the empty space between two moments of satisfaction.

For anyone who suffers from haste—and suffering is here the only correct ethical term, since haste is not chosen—deferment is not just full of blank absurdity; it also carries the menace of crisis. Imposed deferment affects self-evident identity. Haste is the tyranny of self-evident clarity which is always menaced by crisis. This is why the hasty person is sometimes described as (someone) fleeing from himself or from God. And the more man becomes his own measure and possesses in science and technology the means to cultivate successfully his arbitrary, independent activities, the more he must relegate his impotence and passivity to some far corner where they fuse into an explosive remnant.

In this, one might say that the law of contrasting effects prevails. The more I am in a hurry, the greater the speed I wish to attain, the more painful and pronounced deferment becomes. Those who wish to impose peace hastily provoke force; anyone who is absolutely determined to sleep continues to lie awake; anyone who does not want to hear disturbing noises hears them all the more readily and adds his own noise to boot. When we look forward to our holidays, we immediately start to feel tired. Emphasis on the one brings it into contagious proximity with the other. Emphatic prohibition renders the forbidden fruit attractive, and a forceful negation conjures up confirmation.

Identity requires contradiction; any philosophizing that propounds identity and matter-of-factness lives by contradiction. In haste, however, contradiction and nonidentity are not accepted and must impose themselves by force. Haste develops from an incidental agitation into an attitude to life, an ideology tyrannical and cheerless. Haste is anticipating an urgent activity. Force is the highest form of activity, and any civilization which glorifies activity as its highest norm must ipso facto glorify force. Force is every form of impatience with regard to deferment. If we wish to combat it we must not be satisfied with demonstrations against the atomic bomb. The emphasis on this bomb allows all other forms of force the chance to develop freely and, if we regard the effect of behavior as its inmost intent, we must concede that the bomb is condemned only so that force in other guises may flourish. A penetrating study could be devoted to the various subtle forms of force that are cultivated in this manner and that already exist outside this context in our thought and in our ideologies.

In contrast to pausing wonder, haste is a passing-by which misses everything. Despairing of the identity of things it comes to rest where only a technical trace of things remains, in the cave of mediocrity where it bars the way to any progress in thought. People's haste is one of the sources of wonder when the attention of thought is focused upon man and his culture. This haste reveals the absurdity of a culture without enthusiastic contemplation, without pleasure, but filled with violent activity in which zeal replaces desire.

2. *The Sacred Ritardando*

Anyone who talks of practicing free fall should not speak so conceitedly about haste and speed. The interesting thing about free fall is precisely the speed which is quadrupled by a sort of haste from within. Here, however, we are not so much concerned with the fall as with the freedom which is hampered by haste. To restore freedom and make contemplation possible a countermovement from inside out is necessary. While wonder with quadrupled speed attacks what the world takes for granted, the person wondering tends more toward pause and contemplation. The forces of a quadrupling retardation enter into dialogue with the laws of free fall. We must pause awhile by this ritardando with a deliberate and perhaps very vulnerable lyricism. Only thus can wonder avoid force and agitation.

A ritardando is a gradual slowing-down movement. It is a slowing down, not an actual slowness. There is first another tempo, followed by the ritardando. It is not there from the beginning, as slowness can exist from the beginning. The ritardando is a small island in the middle of a movement of a different sort, something apart, independent. The motive force is, as it were, suddenly stricken and brought to a standstill. Admittedly the movement does not cease but it inclines toward ceasing. It is only a movement still insofar as it cannot be a halt. But it no longer passes anything and, in a manner of speaking, absorbs all that it would pass were it a rapid movement, and thus it expands sideways. This means that it is no longer merely a tempo, a line; it is a whole world of meanings, a broadening intensification in the spidery schema of movement where meanings pile up. This gives it an entirely different character.

Tempo is time. Every time has its tempo. Past time and present time each have a tempo. According to Ludwig Klages the movement toward the future is a rapid movement, that from the past a slow one. The tempo of the future is speed; slowness is the tempo of the past. Whoever moves rapidly is preoccupied with the goal of his movement. He knows where he is going. Whoever moves slowly, on the other hand, seems to dwell in thought on the starting point of his movement. A person coming from somewhere usually walks slower than the person going somewhere. One might say that slowness gathers the past into the present.

According as time gives different norms to our thought, awareness of time accelerates or slackens our movements. Where the future is a norm, movements become rapid and speed becomes almost a means to an end in itself. Where the past is the norm, however, movements are slower, almost checked in an attempt to return to that past or at least to verify every part of the action with regard to the past. And the past is a powerful norm, for it is a source of experiences. To have a past is to have experience. Wherever the past is the norm, old age has the greatest authority and imposes the slowness of its thought and movement on the whole community.

Besides this personal old age there is the age of the race. The ancient race that has a long and perhaps a great past is a distinguished race. Nobility is past, and where the past is norm, old age is distinguished. Distinction in this sense means being able to lean upon the past, being part of a safe, historical series. The past is a backrest, a justification of existence, and a fund upon which to draw in the present.

Distinction thus consists in possessing the past and turning toward the past. This turning toward the past appears from one of the most important characteristics of this sort of distinction, which is a dignified slowness, a lofty tempo. To be in a hurry is not distinguished.

"This slowness is suited to great matters" (Vondel). There are various reasons for this. In the first place, the distinguished person is in a position to delegate his movements; he allows himself to be carried. Distinguished Romans had themselves carried by slaves. This was not a rapid mode of transport, nor was it particularly comfortable, but it demonstrated very clearly that they were not obliged to carry out banal movements of their own power. This lofty tempo can be taken very literally. The distinguished are carried not only by their time, the past, but they can also allow themselves to delegate their movements so that they are borne above the common herd. The distinguished person does nothing that he can get others to do for him. He does not dissipate his energy but conserves it for the performance of acts that he alone can do. He concentrates his energy on the real thing. To walk quickly is to invest so much energy in the actual walking that not enough is left for the real work toward which one is moving.

One can allow oneself to be slow, if one can choose one's tempo oneself and let others wait. The slowness so suited to great affairs and distinguished gentlemen develops wherever the importance of an act is bound up to a large extent with the fact that someone is waiting for it. Waiting confers importance on things, and from the time one can make a person wait, one has him in his power. The simple fact of sitting behind a desk or counter is sufficient to slow down a person's movements. One is then in contact with a bureaucratic center where the movement toward this center decreases in pace, comes to a halt almost, anxious, as it were, lest it should not be able to brake in time for the curve backward to the periphery where the matter, now become important, is awaited with impatience. In this way the bureaucrat is the heir to past distinction. His slowness is the offshoot and the relic of a once sacred ritardando.

Another example of bad slowness is rigidity. This is the great danger that menaces slowness, the ritual tempo. There are rapid rites, of which the dance is one. Generally speaking every ritual attempt to achieve the impossible by means of magic will be originally a rapid movement. Rapidity here is a passing-by the means, a bypassing of the reasonable stage in the attempt. Yet these rites too grow slower as they become more institutionalized. It can then happen that this slowness is no longer the hieratic, sacral ritardando that arises from the certainty of being borne by a world ground that can be approached in reverse, but a stagnation. The ritardando then is a movement that has become stylized, that is slow only because there is no force behind it. Not only does it not hasten along a predetermined line to a goal but it does not expand sideways either. It is not based upon a past but floats on under its own power until, obeying the laws of inertia, it grinds completely to a halt. The part which stagnation plays in the ritardando of the rite must not be underestimated.

Running is not distinguished. The distinguished movement is the stride. The stride is a measured, ritual manner of walking. The ritardando is the tempo of the rite. Where the banal moving of various actions from which some benefit is expected ends up as a rite, these movements are retarded. Rare are the rituals that have to be performed quickly, and even then their tempo slackens off in the course of their history. Like the ritardando the rite is an island of slowness in a world of speed, completely different from its surroundings. In the ritardando of movement the subject reserves the movement for itself, refuses to pour out its energy over the world, and makes a world of very movement. This movement goes nowhere but exists for itself. What in walking is the goal toward which one is making is here swallowed up in the movement itself and the act of digestion slows it down.

Distinguished slowness means being certain of one's time. The only time one can possess and of which one is certain is past time. Borne by the past one can allow himself to be slow. One need not go anywhere, one is always already there. The ritardando is the movement of the person with a past of a certain nobility. Haste is, as it were, the fear of being overtaken by time, of being stabbed in the back by it. The distinguished person has time at his back as a reliable ally. He is in no hurry for he has, as they say, the time and indeed the only time one can have, which is the past. The hasty man must overtake time, rush past the future. Only if he were to have the future would he have time. Yet if he could overtake the future, he would not have the future but the past. One cannot have the future; it is the time one does not possess by definition since it lies before us. It has yet to come and this coming can only be awaited, not grasped.

The ritardando is the movement of what is embedded in a past, of something that moves not in order to attain by this movement a certain goal but for the sake of the movement itself which is an encircling of all that it meets on the way. The ritardando is a movement which passes nothing, a marking time. The goal to be attained by this movement is already achieved when the movement begins. This movement, bobbing up and down on the past and already possessing it, is not an attempt to acquire something now, but rather to intensify the possession of the old. It is a possession, a sitting upon, a hatching of what is already there, the intensification of a possessive relationship with regard to what is already present.

In order to acquire something there is no need to go to it. We already have everything. Life is not a roadway, but a marking time. Rapid movement toward something is a bypassing, a denial of all that lies between the point of departure and the goal, between two fictions, and therefore of all that is real. "Alles liegt am Weg," says Heidegger. We are en route for the sake of what lies on the way, not in order to pass it but to possess it. We find nothing new at the end of the road; we have everything then. Or, put it this way: the way is only a detour toward what we already have, the fashion in which we take possession of it, a manner of seeing things one by one but not of reaching them. The way is the deferment of actual identity.

Speed, passing, is a factor that robs life of its meaning. Speed conduces to one-sidedness; to walk hastily is to walk past. Anyone who wants to get far must not walk quickly. Perhaps it is not the walker's fault that he walks past the flowers along the way; perhaps he walks along a road without knowing that other roads exist. Speed is often regarded as a supreme sign of vitality, but it is playing with death. It is incarceration in the narrow one-way flight of the striving for the profitable. There is this too: speed is one of the qualities of flight. It is the panic flight from the nearness of things and from the obligations imposed by this threatening nearness. Slowness is steadfastness, long-suffering, patience, a willingness to suffer from the things that are where we are too.

The ritardando is the tempo of the man who has time and has nothing to fear from the closeness of things. A movement which slows down puts the mover to the test; it confronts him with a multiplicity of things at one and the same time. Slowness is a voluntary crisis in which the moving object focuses its attention and sums up in the one moment of slowness the road it has traveled and all that it has passed on the way. Slowness collects things. Not speed but slowness creates a link between things. Speed draws only arbitrary dotted lines which are soon forgotten. It destroys unity, isolates things, and creates distance. It transforms the deferment into an irremediable diaspora.

Whoever is certain of the purpose of his movement can execute it quickly. Speed then becomes the determination with which he passes whatever lies between the point of departure and the goal. This seems to impart to speed a greater certainty. But what is the quality of this certainty? The ritardando is a hesitation which makes it appear that the movement still has to be designed while it is already being carried out. It seems to slow down, stricken by a sudden uncertainty regarding the road to be followed, while the rapid movement is performed, as it were, mechanically and with accurate self-assurance.

The only rapid movement possible is that which is not an aim in itself, which has to skip something, a movement that exists only because immediacy is impossible. It is only a means. It can never be a festive movement. The certainty that gives rise to it is one of artificial choice, of mechanical orientation toward a tangible goal that can be taken by surprise.

There is a hesitation inherent in the ritardando. There is an art in hesitating, in admitting that we have to consider the next step. A choice without fear for the destruction of the non-chosen possibilities is not an authentic choice. In a certain sense fear is a talent. Hesitation inspired by fear is preferable to the haste which proceeds from a spasm of will. The hasty man has chosen his goal and his road and has decided to pass over all the rest. He rushes along this road like a mechanical toy, and like a toy he is blind. The fear of the slow-moving man is circumspection, a desire to see all sides that create space around a linear movement. He transforms the movement into a way, the line into a space, the journey into a dwelling. Whatever moves slowly dwells in the movement that takes it along the road. The ritardando is the unity of moving, passing, and dwelling. It is the movement that takes with it and absorbs in the mover himself all that is encountered along the road. It implicates everything in its movement.

The ritardando is the tempo of life. The more past a life has, the more content. And the more content it has, the slower it moves. It moves toward a halt, toward a point at which moving and passing have become superfluous. There is a point of satiation and vital completion at which life no longer has a goal but is a goal which can be enjoyed on the spot. Life is filled to the brim with its past. It does not stand still but has reached a climax. It is consecrated (initiated) and need no longer hasten in order to overtake life.

> Alles des Eilende
> wird schon vorüber sein;
> denn das Verweilende
> erst weiht uns ein.
> (Rilke).

Since slowness is a crisis, it takes courage. Heidegger speaks of the "courage of the slow." This courage is linked with respect for things. "Die Scheu hemmt nicht. Aber sie legt das Langsame auf den weg." The hesitation which gives rise to it is the concentration upon what is real (unique), important, and original. "Die Scheu ist das Wissen, dasz der Ursprung sich nicht unmittelbar erfahren läszt." The impatience of speed prevents things from maturing into the fullness of their meaning. Slowness, a slackening of pace, is the adoption of an expectant and wondering attitude toward things. It is not pure passiveness but a suspension of activity. This is why we are said to "pause" in wonder. Wonder necessitates a ritardando in which the new can be digested. During this ritardando the mover becomes filled, as it were, by the world through which he moves, and his eyes are opened to it.

The ritardando is not a halt but a movement in which a tendency to halt is discounted. In this tendency the possibilities passed are celebrated. The ritardando has a festive character. A feast is, as we have said, the solemn emphasis of a positive existence, whose goal lies in itself. The festive ritardando is a pausing by possibilities that may never come to pass but nonetheless are too important to be denied in passing and, in that denial, destroyed and made meaningless. The ritardando is the attitude of a man who travels a road and thus passes along, but in that passing spares and blesses what he passes. It is the circumspection of a movement, of necessity straight and passing through, that enters no road without considering all the possibilities destroyed by this choice, a weighty progress in a spatial encircling, a thinking movement.

"Im Denken wird jeglich Ding einsam und langsam," says Heidegger. Thought retards movement. There is so much to be thought about with regard to every meeting along the way that movement halts to a tarrying. The ritardando is the tempo of thinking movement in which nothing is passed by. Whatever is met on the way is initiated into the totality of what is already present after it has first given rise to a wondering pause in its loneliness and uniqueness. Thinking movement is a way of moving in which a link is established between everything that is passed. Things are weighed and considered and everything that the movement meets weighs along too. Thus the ritardando acquires a weight and a seriousness in which things acquire their meaning and become as it were ripe for their definitive identity.

The thought that accompanies movement and slows it down to a ritardando is a special sort of thought which we call musing. Thought is playing with possibilities, creating space around things. Musing is a game with those possibilities that movement has passed by. Musing is a rehabilitation of passed possibilities, a pondering on how life would have been if not these, but entirely different, possibilities had been realized. Life is necessarily a road; musing restores the space about this road. Or, to put it in a different way: every realization is but a drop which condenses from a cloud of possibilities. Musing senses the cloud that still surrounds the drop, it restores the cloud from which the drop has descended. Wherever choice is necessary you have musing. Choice evokes musing, the nostalgia for lost possibilities. Musing itself is the cloud that surrounds the narrow space of a life filled with toil and choice.

Musing is marking time, a retarded, iterative thought whose goal is not to arrive at certain conclusions but to restore the lost intimacy with things. It is a thinking repetition which serves to render impossible a repetition of actions—which is of itself impossible. It is a constant return to and restoration of the past. In musing, the past is a norm. For this reason too the ritardando is the tempo of musing as it is of the rite which, after all, according to Eliade, is also a return to the past or, rather, over the past toward primeval times. To muse is to think out of and toward the past, to bob about and to be carried by swells toward the past, without method and with no particular route, a *regressus in uterum*, in other words toward the virgin totality of all possibilities, toward a whole identity. Musing, therefore, can be called meaningless, yet it would be wrong to give a pejorative sense to such an elementary necessity. As a choice, musing in that sense is perhaps meaningless: as pathos it cannot be bound by such a qualification.

Yet we can also apply the word "sacred" to this ritardando of movement and thought if we understand it in the sense it originally possessed. The ritardando is born of an anxiety concerning the integrity of the totality of things and possibilities. It allows the totality to exist in its "wholeness," and for this reason it is sacred. Hallowness is wholeness, integrity: to hallow is to heal, make whole, view in the perspective of a restored identity The whole is holy because it is not only whole in the relative sense, without wounds in the totality that is the self, but also "total" in the absolute sense.

In other words what is "whole" is not only that which does not disintegrate, but also that which is "all." It is this wholeness with which the holy ritardando is concerned or, rather, solicitude for the integrity of the whole and an anxiety to preserve the link between things, ideally at least, retard the movement of the scrupulous and thinking man to a ritardando. Since then thought is inconceivable unless the totality is at stake, thought is also impossible without the ritardando. Only retarded thought, musing, is holy thought, wisdom. Without a portion of defenseless passivity, without a realization of its own meaninglessness, wisdom is not what it ought to be.

3. Musing and Action

Contrasted with the unsurmountable scandal of force, musing seems an attitude divorced from this world. It even appears an immoral attitude when it does nothing to decrease the strength of force. Marx's statement that thought ought to change the world is still valid. But musing would appear to be the form of contemplation least likely to change the world and, to this extent, musing thought is just as big a scandal as force.

Musing, however, is one of the extreme forms of thought.

No thinker continues to muse his whole life long. Nor is musing the ideal form of thought, to be preferred above others. Rather is it the form of thought in which the thinker nourishes and stokes himself. Thought contains a dialectic between the extremes of tranquil contemplation and almost palpable action. The wonder which gives rise to it is just as much contemplative as exalted. This is what makes it fitting to be the beginning and principle of philosophy.

To speak or write from the standpoint of wonder already implies the pretension to change the world even where no force is preached. Pretension is a reaching out toward the world, an attempt to get a grip on it. Whoever thinks and writes intends in some way or other to influence the world and the course of world events. Even purely administrative jotting down is a grasp at the world. Every form of literature that uses words and does not merely set them down on paper as objects of desire and contemplation in themselves —roughly Sartre's definition of poetry—reaches through these words toward a reality, and intervenes in the world. But to intervene is to change, and so it may be said that we think and write in order to change the world.

There is material for endless discussion here, even if one agrees that writing does not refer to pure poetry or to the self-contained story but to the account of a process of thought. In my opinion the stretch of time in which the change might be expected could be a criterion in distinguishing various sorts of literature, all engaged to some extent and tainted with pretensions. Literature must be placed upon a scale in deferment and measured by its degree of impatience and force.

Now there is one condition attached to this pretension that is almost incapable of fulfilment, and the type of thinker or writer who sets to work as though this condition were already fulfilled may readily appear naive. In order to change the world it is not enough to understand it; it is more essential to know where things have gone wrong. It is also essential that the thinker should have sufficient confidence in the power of the word in general and of his own words in particular. This will give him the courage to write toward a particular end. Viewed from this endless perspective it is not sufficient to say that the world must change. That everything must become different is an ethical translation of the prime fact granted in wonder: everything is different. Whoever expects or demands more of philosophy than a radicalization of this datum, as Marx evidently does, cannot be satisfied with simply repeating it.

Philosophically speaking, Marx' statement that the philosopher ought to change the world is no new discovery. It is nothing other than the disquiet which Socrates aroused among his fellow men. In itself this stimulus can just as well lead to a mystique of thought and even to softly purring musings such as the Platonic doctrine of Ideas. But Plato too wished to change the world as a philosopher and this was why he desired to see his state governed by philosophers. The philosopher must descend into the cave and free the governors there from their ossified identity. But this very freeing from the cave is described by Plato as an act of force. Certainties are needed here of which no one has the monopoly. No one knows whether the force he wants to use in order to free people from the cave will be the last force, the force to end all force, which in this fact alone can find its justification.

The philosopher thus will tend to think rather toward a "completely different" than toward a clear "thus." The more critical he is with regard to the clarity of that "thus," the more probably he is a philosopher. The only task that remains then is to sow disquiet in the cave. If now we define the writer as a person who possesses the confidence described, then the length of time taken and the clarity of the change remain as criteria for various sorts of authorship and for the limits of seriousness with which it becomes involved in the world. There is thus possible not only a variation between infinitely short and infinitely long but also a variation in the reflection upon one's own expectation from infinitely serious to infinitely frivolous. For it is possible to identify oneself with one's expectations entirely or not at all, and this provides a spectrum of possibilities all of which appear as degrees of patience or impatience. Writing is carried on between distant musing and direct action. Every piece of writing is probably enacted entirely as the movement between these two extremes but for the sake of argument we shall fix certain points on that line. We slow down and classify reality in order to view it better for a moment.

For the rest, our chief concern here is not with types of writing. We are interested in enduring deferment and the manner in which this is done. In haste, deferment is denied and destroyed insofar as possible. To the matter-of-fact person it does not exist. In thought it acquires a perspective of infinity but this infinity is not definitive. From time immemorial thought has also been regarded as a striving toward uniqueness and identity. The usual translation of philosophy is desire for wisdom, but an earlier meaning of the *philos* element is "own." In Homer it is almost a possessive pronoun. Philosophy is also "own wisdom," a movement initiated by man against an encroaching alienation, an attempt to restore identity, to integrate the "other" into the "like." The actual loss of identity lies at the basis of this urge. The factual nature of this loss means that it is irrevocable and unsurmountable which in turn implies that philosophy can never be entirely serious.

The philosopher cannot simply identify himself with an endless and impossible task. There is a limit to seriousness which is naivete. This is revealed in the almost magical expectation that words will have an immediate and total effect upon the world. The word, like an incantation, a curse, or a blessing, must bring about the miracle of immediate change. The word of the magician is the word of absolute impatience; word and expectation are identical. There is no distance of contemplation or intent and thus no free space in which literature may emerge. The magical word itself is *hinfällig*, it is only a pregnant sound.

The more impatient a thinker is, the more clearly he sees the end term of his expectation, the more naive he is and the more easily transformed into an agitator who is so absorbed in the realization of his projects that he leaves himself no room to maneuver. This room is the space of the actual deferment that is endured. It is clear proof of the unrivaled greatness of Plato as a philosopher that, although brimful of clear political ideals, he could set them down in a playful manner. Nor is his game an indifference, assumed or cultivated in order to make the deferment bearable and to banish boredom. It is itself a dwelling in the deferment and thus not something that can be grafted onto philosophy from outside. Plato's game vibrates within the field of tension of his actual thought. As a philosopher he cannot be an agitator without becoming hopelessly alienated from himself.

The same applies to the artist. The inexorable demands of independence and autonomy imposed by art imply that it cannot accept any identity thrust upon it from outside. To the agitator literature and thought are incidentals, interspersed by great deeds and forceful action, inspired by a clear and too hastily identified image of reality as it ought to be. Angry, greedy, grasping at truth deforms truth and the person grasping at it. It makes its own limited truths—slogans.

The vehement, moralizing, preaching authors, the tormented souls searching for nothing less than the full truth all at once and for the meaning of existence, may therefore perhaps be interesting as personalities, but the very qualities that make them interesting as individuals are those that prevent their work from bearing fruit. Their vehemence inserts itself between them and the truth and becomes something of an independent order. Measured by its objective significance the relationship of the interesting to the truth probably resembles that of the incidental to the structural. It may be that here one meets a person, a consistent and fascinating existence, but this usually leads to a rather wishy-washy veneration which seems doomed to a sudden decline for the elementary reason that the meeting on which it is based is more a confrontation with one of the problematic sides of one's own existence than with a chunk of reality.

A thinker who, when all is said and done, invites interest in his own personality only because he is unable to grasp reality, and is only a prophet, rebel, mystic or lyric poet, allows his work to evaporate in the heat which he generates. He becomes a glowing piece of haste and arbitrariness. His admirer can more easily become his biographer than adopt and carry on his aims. For the life and history of such a thinker may at least be approached with some degree of objectivity and one remains in a certain manner close to his ideals. It has indeed been said that life and work are closely linked, and this statement holds a modicum of truth for authors of this kind.

Yet if the work presents no other reality than the incidental character and history of its author, it is at best only second rate. In a certain sense, one degrades the work by associating it so closely with the character and fortunes of the author. Heidegger, who admires Aristotle intensely, sums up his entire biography in the words: "He was born, worked, and died," a biography which for all its brevity is also completely superfluous, since it is the biography of every man who ever lived. We quote it here only to indicate that the greatest significance must be attributed to the actual work.

Aristotle is a writer of infinite academic patience, and his grasp of the world was firmer the less hasty he was. For this reason work is to be preferred to the individual. It deals directly with reality. A biography is of no significance here; it would assume that it is the personality of the thinker that changes the world as an independent medium, not the manner in which he formulates his thought. The biography would appear to be a literary genre having no immediate connection with thought insofar as thought nourishes the pretension of being able to change the world.

In this respect too Plato is a thinker and writer without equal, who seems to make game of all the rules. His thought is by no means arbitrary, whereas he nonetheless urges that the world should be changed. It is moreover of the

purest philosophical quality while remaining strongly bio-
graphical. Plato's work is a biography of Socrates. In nearly
all the dialogues it is not Plato himself speaking, but
Socrates. Plato is the greatest philosopher simply by being
the biographer of a man who preached only disquiet, ignorance, and wonder, who wanted everything changed but
was unable to say how. This would seem a dubious basis
for a philosophical oeuvre, but then Plato was the philosopher who made it possible to dwell in deferment and was
therefore able to renounce all forms of agitation.

Agitation goes beyond the bounds of philosophizing since
it is a form of haste, impatience, and force. The certainty
that everything is different does not imply knowledge concerning the exact quality of that "difference" but on the
contrary excludes it. When philosophical unrest seeks an
outlet in political activity and revolution it becomes alienated from itself. This disquiet must exist in order to give
to thought its philosophical content, but it must not be
surmounted in the execution of a concrete plan. It is not
the philosopher's task to reform the world, but to prevent it
from assuming a rigid identity and becoming a cave. This is
the task given to him in wonder and thus far did Plato go
on the inspiration of Socrates.

There are also philosophers who possess little patience:
the Russian Berdyaev was one of them. Van Gelre calls
his philosophy an "uninterrupted protest against the world
as an unchangeable fact." It might be said that he shares
this trait with all philosophers, from Socrates onward: this
is what makes him a philosopher. But Berdyaev is impatience personified. He himself calls this his weakest point;
he is a philosopher of impatience, of haste, and of the short
term. This made him an interesting, tormented, and constantly prophesying figure and filled his work with diffuse
and pretentious expositions all jumbled up together, dealing
with so many things and so much history at once that they
degenerate into meaningless phrases, the buzzing accompaniment of a desire to reform and to influence, which
remains too undisciplined and too impatient to achieve a
confrontation with even one aspect of reality.

Berdyaev wants to do too much as a philosopher; he wants to achieve what all men working together in perfect harmony would scarcely be able to accomplish. He even wants to break through the force of the general and thus do away with the deferment of identity. He can for instance write: "Nothing 'general' is capable of consoling the 'individual' being in his happy fate." This is a noble and impressive statement which testifies to a considerable degree of humanitarianism but, remarkably enough, it is precisely its general nature that makes it so impressive and consoling. We can expect nothing better of science and philosophy than general statements, the culmination of an infinite patience and detachment viewed as a matter of principle. For the concrete nature of man's need is shattering.

Space can only be created by denying identity or by postponing it indefinitely in the affirmation of the idea and of the general. And this is precisely what the general does, which explains why only the general can offer any consolation. The structure of the consoling, the encircling, is general. I suffer only so long as I identify myself with suffering and can give it no general significance. And as long as I suffer in this way, I do not understand my own suffering. It is this that might inspire the philosopher to force, were he not aware that force in this respect is meaningless. He desires to contrast with himself the anonymous suffering which lies shattered upon its own identity and therefore cannot recognize itself, and to give it a place in the infinite deferment.

The philosopher interprets the identity of people in the cave as suffering; his wonder is easily transformed into sympathy with an existence which is incapable of interpreting itself and thus easily falls prey to the exploiter. In this way the consolation of philosophy can degenerate into force and even become exploitation. One might say that it desires suffering so as to be able to preach liberation. Compassion is based upon an interpretation of a situation that is not experienced as suffering but as a normal condition, a pure undergoing and going under without any dialectic with man's independent nature. Compassion might almost be considered a form of force since it breeds rebellion. As such it is a philosophical force, the laying of a fuse in the identity of an impotent existence. Compassion is the unsurmountable arrogance of philosophical thought.

If everything is different, this fact has its caustic effect both upward and downward. It influences the joy and enthusiasm upon which a perspective is opened and also the suffering which is essential for a proper functioning of the dialectic. Suffering and need themselves thus are also general in the eyes of the philosopher, a principle of mobility which justifies his disquiet. For this reason Spinoza and Hegel offer more consolation than do Kierkegaard and Berdyaev. For them the general is the "other," in its liberating, space-making form. The "other" is necessary for comfort and liberation, especially in its free, contemplative, and most patient guise, not disformed by any arbitary intervention on my own part. The consolation of the general does not intervene immediately in suffering, caviling and heavy-handed, but allows it to retain its own being and points out to it an infinitely deferred identity.

Whatever I can find in myself I must willingly renew every moment as a precarious faith that I may lose again at any moment. One needs such a faith in order to console oneself by one's own powers, without the general. Yet this faith requires a mental robustness that people in need cannot be assumed to possess and its permanent production is infinitely more tiring and saddening than resignation to the general. The ethics of bravery and independence fail nowhere so glaringly as where it reveals its origin in impatience, namely when faced with the defenselessness of suffering. It is for this reason that the arbitrarily chosen principle appeals least of all to the person in real need. In absolutely defenseless passivity that which is less of a choice and more of a gift seems to be the most inalienable possession.

The time limit of expectation with which we meet the world in thought may be indefinite. The paradoxical thing is that the most academic and disinterested patience has the tightest grip on the world and that the acceptance of deferment makes suffering bearable. The person who resists pain, feels only more pain. No writer has influenced the world more than the most objective philosopher. The most basic change in reality proceeds directly from an insight into its character. The most radical revolutions are not the product of political agitation but of scientific, disinterested views acquired patiently and in obedience to matter. No raucous cries for revolution and no crafty reasoning in favor of preservation have had a fraction of the historical significance which the patient and disinterested exploration of the possibilities inherent in matter and society has had and continues to have.

The philosopher in his study does not hold aloof from reality and Berdyaev was enough of a philosopher to remain working at his writing table during the outbreak of the Russian revolution. Kant and Hegel would have done the same, and it is said of Socrates that he stood for hours in contemplation on the battlefield. Here we have no facile contrast between theory and practice or between ideal and reality but rather a refractory identity of wonder and outrage. Thought itself is an aggression against reality. To think is to be aware of alienation. The philosopher does not set up for himself an arbitrary and artificial ideal to which he aspires to convert the world. His thought itself is revolutionary and ethical in inspiration since it is aimed at the optimal realization of possibilities and indicates the existence of a world outside the cave. This world is not a different world outside this world, but an optimal realization of this world.

The eschatological perspective of every philosophy lies within the one world at which it is aimed, not in a mythical world outside or in a post-historical era. It is a way of seeing and experiencing things rather than one of effort and accomplishment. The tension peculiar to a philosophical work lies within the identity of the object itself. Philosophy is that tension; for her there is no outlet.

DATE DUE

3/v/			
SEP 3 0 1979			
GAYLORD			PRINTED IN U.S.A.